# THE H                    I

## A Journey into the Light

An Inspiring True Story of Transformation
From Courage and Survival to Forgiveness and Love

# EDEN REIN

## FOREWORD BY EARLENE VINING

EDEN REIN
PUBLISHING

Cover and logo/imprint design by Mitch Mahoney at
www.euphoricmedia.net

Interior design by Eden Rein

ISBN-10:  0615997619
ISBN-13:  978-0615997612

Eden Rein Publishing
www.edenrein.com

*This book is dedicated*
*to the children of the world*
*and*
*to my nephews Lochlan and McCoy*

# CONTENTS

# FOREWORD

I first met Eden Rein on June 16, 2012, in Vancouver, BC, Canada. She was a dynamic participant in a personal development seminar that I was conducting for the Global Information Network.

During the program, there were several sessions that provided the participants an opportunity to share a story about themselves and their achievements. Eden was quick to volunteer to speak during those sessions. She exhibited a confidence that made her a stand-out in the class as a very articulate, attractive, and intelligent woman. I enjoyed visiting with Eden during some of the breaks and was impressed that she was a woman who was determined to follow her dreams.

Several months later, Eden told me she had written a book about her journey through a difficult childhood. She explained that she wanted to publish this book to help others who may have been born into similar circumstances or perhaps have had similar experiences.

As I read through the pages of her manuscript, I was inspired by the courage, determination, and tenacity that Eden was blessed with. These traits helped her to survive extreme challenges that she endured throughout her childhood.

Eden will explain in her story that she was born in Vietnam, but moved several times due to her father's being in the military. Like most little girls, Eden wanted to be loved, nurtured and respected by her parents. Her story will reveal that she never experienced affection or received any sign of love from her mother. At a very early age, Eden was given far too many responsibilities, as she became a full-time babysitter to her brothers, a housekeeper, and a caretaker. Eden hungered for some positive recognition, but instead was constantly criticized by her mother and often physically beaten. Finally, she found herself struggling in the painful trenches of darkness, with a very low self-esteem. She felt ugly and very alone. You will be amazed and inspired by her "will" to survive. Eden could easily have chosen to stay in this dark place, but instead, she kept a strong faith which helped her to focus on love and forgiveness. These two characteristics guided her on a path to success and happiness. She chose not to be a victim, but rather, an example of transformation from darkness to the light. Congratulations Eden! You are truly one of my Heroes. I am honored to be one of your friends and mentors.

Earlene Vining, President
Bee Creative, Inc.
Vice President and Co-Founder
Executive Development Systems, Inc. and
The SUCCESSFUL LIFE Course
Author, Speaker, Trainer
Mother of three

# PREFACE

I have known for many years that I should write a memoir. It was just a feeling I had. Then I began meeting people who told me I should write about my experiences. Yet there were fears, fear of what people would think and fear of people recognizing me. Thankfully, I overcame those fears and tapped into a source that everything we do should originate from—Love. The desire to inspire and help others overshadowed my imagined discomforts and propelled me to finally take action.

My purpose in writing this memoir therefore is to inspire others to write their story or to achieve any endeavor they desire, regardless of would be naysayers or potential critics. This requires determination and imagination. One of my favorite quotes on imagination comes from Albert Einstein: "Logic will get you from A to B. Imagination will take you everywhere."

I urge you that no matter whom you are and no matter what your current circumstances, if you have a dream, just go for it. Do not delay, do not wait, do not hesitate, and do not procrastinate, for you may someday find that it might be too late. Because if you don't act now, you may find that someday soon, someone else who has received that same idea that you did, has taken action and made their dream come true. I have spoken to many people who have seen their dreams and ideas snatched from their minds, so to speak, and seen its reality fulfilled by someone else.

A good example of this is when I was thinking of what I wanted to title my book. The title that came to me when I began my writing late in 2011 was "The Hero Within," which I thought was an original. As I did some research however, I found that there were already a couple of books with that title;

however, none of them were memoirs. Then in 2012, I didn't write because I was distracted with looking for a job and paying bills, thinking that was what I needed to do. I was wrong. That year, because I didn't do what I knew I was supposed to be doing, another book was published with that same title. Even though it wasn't a memoir, I immediately saw the writing on the wall and *got the message*. The Universe or God gives you signs and signals and if you don't accept these gifts with gratitude by acting upon them, the Universe will give it to somebody else who will. Fortunately for me, I had a burning desire to write my story so I remained undeterred. There was no way I was going to give up!

When it comes to your dreams, if you are concerned about not having the money or people to help you, my experience has been, what I have been taught, and what I have seen many others do, is to just focus on what it is that you desire. That is really all you have to do. It's simple but I know for many people, including myself at times, it is difficult to do. Yet I know it works. Just keep focused on and imagine the outcome of what it is that you want and everything will fall into place. The circumstances, funds, and people will all appear as if by magic.

This concept is not new of course and I know many readers will be able to recognize its various origins. It's no secret. While writing this memoir, I have been simultaneously reading *The Law of Success* by Napoleon Hill, the original 1925 edition, which has had tremendous impact on my thinking and tremendous influence on the fruition of my dream. I was also inspired by the CD series, "Your Wish Is Your Command." I highly recommend listening to that CD series and reading *The Law of Success* and also *Think and Grow Rich* by Napoleon Hill. Books like these and other factors, such as aligning yourself with like-minded people who will support you is *essential* to the attainment of your dreams.

If you do not quite know what your dream is or what it is that you desire, this story and message may help you find it. It's here to help you listen to that inner voice and higher calling that may just only be a faint whisper. But no matter who you are, you have a purpose. It doesn't matter where you begin, even if it's at below zero like I was, you can rise above it all and achieve great heights toward that purpose and toward that dream. Just do it!

## The Readers

When I began writing I thought I would mainly be writing to women audiences. However, I began meeting men whom I felt could benefit from my story as well. Soon, my vision for my audience and readers started to expand. So here they now are: women, Asian Americans, Veterans of the Vietnam War, teenagers, orphans, anyone who grew up in a dysfunctional home, anyone who was adopted, anyone who is interested in learning about other cultures, anyone who is interested in personal growth—virtually everyone.

## Names of Characters

As the reader of this or any other memoir would understand, the names have been changed to protect their identity, including my own. During this process of recalling my experiences, I found that I have actually forgotten some of the names of the people I have connected with over the years. Therefore, the selection of a name for a character that was actually the real name of that individual was not intentional.

While I've come to learn that everything is energy, including our names, it is my intention that the surrounding context of the story aside from the names will provide the reader with the true message that is being conveyed. Especially since among the Vietnamese, names are very important and have special meanings, which I didn't understand growing up. This was due to my inability to communicate with my mother in Vietnamese and her inability to fully explain to me in English the translation for many things, including name meanings. Because of our inability to understand each other, it led to a lot of frustration for both of us. For example, when I was learning a lot of new words in school and increasing my vocabulary, I became frustrated with her because I knew I could never use those words at home. The few times I did use a new word with my mother, she of course didn't understand and I would end up just saying, "Never mind."

The name Luc is actually a French name and is similar to the spelling of my older brother's name that he went by except for one letter. His given name and the one on his birth certificate were not what we used to address him. Similarly James (not his real name), one of my younger brothers was actually given a Vietnamese name at birth. However, we did not address him by his Vietnamese name but called him by his American name, which he later legally changed it to as an adult. This was probably due to his lack of understanding or knowing the meaning of his given name. In addition, growing up in a small predominantly Caucasian town in California where there were very few Asians, the desire to fit in with the other kids made it less conducive to accept and embrace the Vietnamese name given to him and to me.

**The Subtitle**

In my search for a subtitle, several concepts and themes came to me; however, the one that stuck had to do with "light".

When I began revealing the subtitle to some of my friends, acquaintances and even strangers, the response was surprisingly favorable, positive, and affirming. There was no explanation needed. However, for the sake of eliminating any enigmatic ideas, a few metaphors may help in revealing the message I wish to convey. What I have experienced and learned about the darkness, as in the dark side of the force or dark energy, is that emotions such as anger, hatred, envy, fear, greed, jealousy, and depression all reside there. The dark is where you feel lost and hopeless.

Whereas the light, as in "the light at the end of the tunnel" or the light of a candle that extinguishes the darkness or the sun's light that breaks the night, holds the lighter emotions of love, happiness, bliss, joy, euphoria, gratitude, forgiveness, and inspiration. Admittedly, I came from a dark place. This was from my mother who sadly didn't love herself so she was incapable of showing love to me and the rest of her family. This was because she wasn't taught to love herself. She just didn't know.

However, at a young age, I chose to go towards the light. I didn't realize it at the time but when I made that decision, I had actually chosen to break that cycle of perpetuating darkness in the family line. As you read through the story, see if you can determine when that took place.

This is not to say I never experienced or felt any negative emotions. Because of my "story", I have experienced many negative emotions for far too long. However, I refused to let them consume me and define who I am. I would not let them influence me to treat others with hatred and anger as I had been taught. The few people I have shared my experiences and story with along my life's journey are astonished with the person I've become and the person I am. They are amazed at how I can be warm and loving, considering where I came from. Yet I realize it was a choice and a decision. We all have choices. I hope you will make the right choice by going towards the light and taking action towards fulfilling your dreams.

# ACKNOWLEDGEMENTS

I am truly grateful and thankful for Henry Eccleston, Eli Rook, Glenn Hardaway, Kevin Trudeau, the Global Information Network (GIN) speakers, the training I received through GIN, and all my GIN friends for without them, this writing and book would not exist. At least not at this moment in time. Because this is a work that had been on my mind to do for many years but I had kept putting off. But it *had* to be done and the time to do it is NOW, or I would have gone to my grave like billions of people on this planet full of regret that I had not done what I knew with every fiber and atom of my being I was designed and destined to do. I am truly grateful for not only their encouragement, guidance, and support, but also their selfless desire to see me live out my dreams and fulfill my destiny.

I thank Elizabeth Farr for her insight and edits on the Afterword. Her belief in me added to the fuel I needed to persist in this work. Special thanks to Henry Eccleston for not only being one of my biggest cheerleaders, but also for not accepting less from me than the materialization of this writing. For in his words I found the impetus and drive to not only commence this work, but also to carry on and bring this work to fulfillment, "You must tell your story! Do you know how many people you can help by telling your story!?"

# INTRODUCTION

You are not a victim. No matter what you've been through and no matter what you're going through now, you are not the victim you thought you were or think you are. You are a hero and in control of your life. There is nothing you can do about the past, except to learn from it, but there are certainly things you can do now, today, that will catapult you into happiness and bliss; the happiness that you desire and the happiness that you deserve. It starts with finding the hero within you, the hero that you are, and the hero you have always been.

Have you ever been asked, "Who inspires you the most?" If you haven't, you've probably seen or heard interviews on television or radio shows of celebrities being asked that question. Perhaps it was an actor, musician, or an athlete, who was being interviewed and often, if it's an actor, they will talk about the films and movies they've seen as a child and they will name the actors they watched on the big screen that inspired them. If it's a musician, they'll list the names of other musicians and bands, and the type of music that they've listened to growing up that inspired them. And of course, in the case of athletes, they too, will name the athletes of former days that they aspire to. But what about the rest of us who aren't actors, famous musicians, or athletes? It seems that we all had someone we looked up to and admired because of their accomplishments and sometimes, as in the case of movie stars and actors, we admire and even idolize them just because they are attractive and beautiful. When it comes to people involved with philanthropy, we applaud them because of the good that they've done for many other people, and we often think of them as heroes. Especially in the case of soldiers, who are on the battle grounds of foreign land, fighting for our safety and security. Certainly, these ones could be considered heroes.

However, have you ever thought for a moment that you are a hero as well? If you are a parent, you might think that your children look up to you as being their hero. If you've been a mentor to someone, perhaps at work or in volunteer work, you may be someone's hero by being a coach, counselor, older brother or sister. Yet, those definitions and roles of being a hero are self evident and obvious to see. What I'm referring to is the recognition of yourself as your own rescuer, your own hero. After all, you've probably experienced a lot of adversities and obstacles in your life and somehow, you are still here, alive, breathing, existing, and perhaps may even be happy and content. If you are not happy, content, or satisfied with your life, this story will show you how it is possible to achieve contentment, happiness, and yes, even bliss despite extraordinary circumstances.

Over the years I have heard many stories of people who have had a dysfunctional, horrific, and abusive childhood. I've heard these stories because of having moved around a lot not only as a child due to my father being in the military but also as an adult. At last count, I have lived in over 30 different homes from birth until the writing of this book. Because of having moved numerous times, I have met many people who have shared their stories and experiences with me.

So while I share my story here, it is my sincere desire to convey to you that this is your story as well or can be your story. This is because it is not the biography of a celebrity, professional athlete, or well known musician, who overcame adversities as a child and then grew up to achieve great fame and stardom. While these are all great and inspiring stories, most people cannot relate to them because they did not achieve or have not yet achieved at the level of success that these celebrities did. Perhaps many people can relate to the experience that the well known celebrity had during his or her childhood, but then to turn that around and achieve the extraordinary things the celebrity did is where most people will draw the line. At that point, they naturally stop relating to that celebrity or sports figure that they idolize or admire. What made it possible for things to all of a sudden seem to turn around for them? They seemed to meet the right people at the right time, where the rest of us continued on to live mediocre lives, despite having experienced similar things during childhood.

Nevertheless, if there is a desire to achieve the same greatness and accomplishments as these celebrities, it is not too late. It is never too late to make that shift and transform yourself into the person you've always wanted to be or to do the things you've always wanted to do. There is no need to give up. Time will pass you by, with or without you. You can continue to do the things you've always done and be the same person you've always been or you can emerge like a butterfly from its cocoon, ready to show the world the beauty and power that is within you.

As a first step towards that person you want to be or were actually born to be, I encourage you to see the greatness that you already are. I hope this story of an ordinary woman's courage, fears, persistence, and survival, will inspire you to see the greatness, the genius, and the hero that is also within you.

A note to parents: I speak of being a hero to your children; however, I would be remiss if I didn't add that you are also their mentor and leader, with the emphasis on leadership. One of the best descriptions of the type of leader you want to be is found in the book, "The Law of Success," by Napoleon Hill. In Lesson Three, Napoleon Hill mentions that there are two types or brands of leaders. There is the deadly brand, "which leads not to *success* but to *absolute failure*, is the brand adopted by pseudo leaders who *force* their leadership on unwilling followers."

Yes, you are the parent and as such you are in charge of guiding or leading your children to success or failure. Your children are your followers, so make sure you lead them to "self-determination and freedom and self-development and enlightenment and justice," which was the brand of leadership that Napoleon Hill recommended.

As you read my story, you will certainly see a description of the leadership style that is certainly not recommended by Napoleon Hill. Fortunately, I was able to find and learn from the leaders that Napoleon did recommend. And I will be forever grateful for their exceptional example of leadership.

Eden Rein
November 13, 2011

# 1 The Ugly Duckling

The Vietnam War had been going on for 10 years. John F. Kennedy was assassinated on November 22, 1963. In 1964 the Beatles conquered the largest record market–America. I was the second child to my mother, who was 17 when she had me and who was 15 when she had my older brother Luc. She had a third child at age 19, by a different husband. Her second husband, the father who raised me, was an American serving in the U.S. Air Force, but who was originally from Germany. My mother met him through some friends when I was 11 months old. She was working in Nga Trang and would send money home to my grandmother who lived in Saigon (now Ho Chi Minh City) and who took care of me and my older brother Luc.

I never knew my biological father and didn't find out that my American father was my stepfather until I was eight. My childhood friend Melissa told me one day, "You know your father isn't your real father. He's your stepfather." That was all she had to say. I knew immediately what she meant, even though I'd never heard the word "stepfather" before. I replied, "So," as I shrugged my shoulders. In that moment, I made up my mind that even though he was not my "real father", I wasn't going to let that bother me. He was the only father I knew and somehow I just felt that he would always be there for me.

As a child, I was very perceptive and noticed things in detail, especially facial features. I realized that I didn't look like my mother but I didn't look like my father either. I had often wondered why. So when my friend Melissa revealed to me that my dad was my stepfather, things just immediately clicked. That explained why I didn't look like a blend of my mother and father, which for some reason I knew I should. My father was fair and had big round blue eyes, with graying brown wavy hair. Mom was also very fair skinned with dark brown hair, almost black and her nose ended in a point instead of being round like mine. The first time I saw the actress Meryl Streep in Kramer vs. Kramer, I thought she reminded me of Mom because of her triangle shaped nose and the shape of her lips.

When we went to church, people would often compliment Mom on her beauty and how nice she looked. Dad said that people would tell him that his wife must have something else in her besides Vietnamese. That was because Vietnam was colonized by the French during the mid 19th century. Many Vietnamese had French mixed in them and many of them spoke French. Even the Vietnamese language, while it may not sound similar, has many words similar to those found in the French language. Although Mom didn't speak French, she was able to read and write in both English and Vietnamese. I later found out that on her father's side, there was a French man that married into the family.

I was the darkest one in my family and for some reason, it made me feel inferior. I'm not sure why I felt that way. Perhaps it was just things I overheard adults say or how they treated me. When we lived in the Philippines, I would tan very easily, whereas my younger brother James remained very pale. Even with living in the tropical Philippines, he still wouldn't tan. I recall one day Mom and Dad were rubbing QT tanning lotion on James in the bathroom. The bathroom door was open so I can see what they were doing and hear what they were saying.

"He so pale! He look sick. We need put this on him so he don't look so sick," Mom said in her broken English.

Even my older brother Luc was fair like my mother. I had heard Mom say that my brother Luc looked like one of her brothers. Evidently he took after Mom's side of the family in appearance instead of my biological father's side. Later, I realized that he also took after Mom in temperament.

In my younger years, I never had any desire to seek out my biological father. Why would I seek out a man who abandoned my mother, not once but twice after getting her pregnant? The story I had heard from my childhood friend Melissa, who was two years older than me, was that my Vietnamese biological father had left Mom after she became pregnant with Luc. Then about two years later, he returned to her and left again, after she became pregnant with me. When I heard that story, I thought what a jerk he was for abandoning Mom that way. I swore I would have nothing to do with him. Why would he and how could he do such a thing? According to Mom, my biological father was ten years older than her and when he would leave her, she felt very lonely and heartbroken.

Another reason why I had no desire to seek out my biological father while growing up was because I felt that my dad would always be there for me; at least he was when I was younger. Yet over time as an adult, my desire to find my biological father grew stronger and stronger. Yet, with only a black and white picture of him when he was in his twenties, given to me by Mom when I had reached adulthood, it seemed impossible to find him. People offered all kinds of suggestions. "You can post his picture on Facebook and I'm sure someone would recognize him," someone suggested. A friend, whose father works for Homeland Security, told me that her father could possibly locate my biological father, but without a name, it would be difficult or impossible to know where to start.

One day I asked Dad about my biological father. I felt a little uneasy doing that because I didn't want Dad to think that I didn't appreciate the things he had done for me, but I needed some answers. He told me that Mom had told him that her first husband, my biological father, had worked for the CIA. That was the first time I heard anyone refer to my biological father as Mom's first husband. I'd always thought he was just a lover or boyfriend. I asked Dad about that, "Oh, he was her first husband?"

Dad explained that back in those days in Vietnam, as soon as two people lived together, they were pretty much considered married. It wasn't necessary for them to get a marriage license because it would cost a lot of money. How sad, I thought, that they didn't have a traditional wedding ceremony. Were they that young and poor that they couldn't even get a marriage license? However, that wasn't the first time I'd heard that my biological father worked for the CIA. My brother James also told me that as well. He had a conversation with Mom one day and asked her several questions regarding my biological father and also, why she had it out for me. Even *he* noticed that she was especially hard on me compared to him and my other brothers.

"Why were you so angry at Eden all the time?" he asked.

"What was it about her that made you mad at her all the time?"

According to James, Mom just looked at him. Either she didn't know what to say because she hadn't realized that's how she had been or she didn't know how to explain it to him. It didn't matter though. I knew why she was harder on me than my brothers. I was surprised that James had the courage to ask Mom about these things and equally surprised she didn't get angry or upset with him for asking her those questions. I know that I wouldn't have had the courage to ask her.

As for my biological father being in the CIA, perhaps that explained why he kept disappearing and why on my birth certificate under Father, it said, "unknown" as translated into

English from Vietnamese. Mom had to have known the name of her husband and the man who fathered two of her children. Why was there no name? Was he really with the CIA? If so, perhaps she didn't put a name down to protect his identity. Or was it because she was ashamed? I had no choice but to believe that he was working for the famous spy agency. What did he do for the CIA? I asked Dad whose side my biological father worked for. Dad told me that he worked for both sides, the U.S. and for Vietnam. I didn't understand. Could he possibly be a double agent and lived a life of adventure? My imagination ran wild.

I continued to wonder. What qualities did I inherit from him? If he indeed really worked for the CIA, then maybe that explained where my intelligence came from. My deduction was not from a place of ego but rather, a way of putting the puzzle pieces together. Growing up, I'd always felt that I was very different from the rest of my family in many ways, including intellectually. But the full impact of this awareness didn't come until years later when I would get bored with my jobs and had to seek out the next challenge or adventure. I would also wonder if there might have been something else that I could have done career wise. Finding out that I may have inherited my biological father's intelligence made me regret the work and career path that I had chosen. I would think to myself, *You mean I could have been a journalist, a doctor or even a lawyer?!* It was a wonder that I was able to achieve the success that I did since I was never taught to believe in myself or to think I could do anything great in this world. Instead, I drifted aimlessly going here and there based on what other people suggested I do, instead of knowing what I wanted to do myself.

Often, I felt that I was smarter than my parents and did well in school without trying too hard. I was an above average student and knew if I really applied myself, I could always get straight A's, which I did in my later high school years. But why bother? It wasn't as if my parents really cared about my grades. During the school year they never asked how I was doing or if I needed any help. If I did well, it was because I wanted to have something I could feel good about. Something to show for my efforts because at home, nothing that I did was ever good enough. I was never thanked for all the cooking, cleaning, and helping with my younger brother's homework. In fact, I *had* to do all those things because if I didn't, I would get beaten. I also wanted to do well because of the friends I seemed to attract. Somehow, I was looked upon as being smart and so I tended to hang out with other kids that were smart too.

However, when it was report card time, that's when it mattered. For every A, we received one dollar and for every B, we received fifty cents. I found it confusing because on the one hand they never got involved with any school activities or meetings. They never went to any parent-teacher conferences and during the school year, never asked how we were doing in school. Dad was too busy working and going to school at night and Mom was too busy socializing with her friends. But then on report card day, all of a sudden, our grades were important.

As a child, I would imagine my biological father was still living in Vietnam and unable to speak English. However, that image changed when in recent years, I learned from my stepmother, Anne, that my biological father was an interpreter. "I don't know who he worked for but I do know he was an interpreter." Mom told Anne that my biological father would come in to town and visit her, but then would leave for long periods of time for his job. Although she didn't know where he would go, she knew he was paid well.

After my biological father was gone for good, according to Anne, Mom told her that he did come back after I was born to see her, see how my brother and I were doing, and to give her a large sum of money, up to $10,000, which was a lot of money back then, especially in Vietnam. However, Mom's family told him to leave her alone because he had done enough damage, so he never saw her again. When I asked Dad about my biological father, he confirmed that my biological father did search for Mom again years later but was told that she was now living in the U.S.

When my biological father left Mom again after she became pregnant with me, she realized that he wasn't coming back or that he wasn't someone she could depend on. So it didn't take her long to move on. And that's when she met my stepfather, whom I have always referred to as my dad and still do. He was the only father I ever knew so to introduce him or to refer to him as my stepfather seemed unnatural. I quickly learned that anyone could bring a child into the world but not everyone can be a father.

Whenever Dad wanted to take pictures of James and me, I was reluctant. One time, my parents took James and me to a stable on base where we could ride ponies. Although I wanted to ride a pony, I didn't want to have my picture taken. I kept protesting that I didn't want to have my picture taken and even cried. My parents couldn't understand why. Of course, I didn't know why either. I just couldn't articulate and communicate to them how ugly and insecure I felt. As I watched James, who had no problem with taking a picture, ride the pony, I realized that I had cheated myself out of a really fun time and lost out on riding a pony. Finally, when Dad explained that he wanted pictures to send to his parents in Germany, my grandparents, I finally gave in. By that time, my eyes were all swollen and although I tried to force a smile, I could see how puffy my eyes were in the photographs.

To add to my insecurity, some school kids in the first grade teased me for having chicken pox scars. The kids would laugh and say, "You have holes on your face!"

I asked Dad about that, "Dad, how come I have these holes on my face? The kids at school are teasing me about them."

"That's because when you were little, you had the chicken pox and nobody was watching you when you were scratching your face. Don't worry, when you get older they will go away," he assured me.

I was relieved to know that the chicken pox scars would fade when I got older, but they didn't. I actually got the chicken pox twice. The first time, I was too young to remember and the second time, I was around six. The scars, I believe, came after the first bout, and it made me sad to know that nobody had been watching me. I had already been feeling neglected, unloved, and unwanted, even though I didn't have the vocabulary for those words.

As a baby, I guess I felt sad quite often. Mom would relate how I cried a lot. When I would hear her say that, I would think, *Hmmm, I wonder why. Maybe it was because I didn't feel loved?*

Perhaps another reason why I felt ugly is because Mom always kept my hair short. She never let my hair grow out long and was always putting curlers in it or having it permed. I remember her taking me to a hairdresser who worked out of her home to get my hair cut and permed. Back then, the permanent solutions were much stronger than they are today. As I sat there waiting for the solution to set, I would gag from the powerful smell of ammonia and thought I was going to die because I couldn't breathe. I also had a very sensitive head and when the hairdresser took the rods out to wash my hair, she was so rough, it made my head hurt. As she yanked the rods free and then washed the solution out, she kept pulling my hair. It was so painful that it brought tears to my eyes. I thought I was going to be bald by the time she was through. I asked Mom why she wouldn't let my hair grow out and why she was always having it cut and curled. She said, "Because I don't want brush your hair. I don't want take care your hair."

One time, my parents took James and me to see Santa Claus and have our pictures taken. I didn't want to go because I had rollers in my hair. However, I couldn't get out of it. Mom didn't feel the need to take the rollers out and insisted that I get my picture taken. I felt so embarrassed. I wondered if she just didn't want me to look pretty. I don't know at exactly what age it was but eventually she stopped having my hair cut short and let it grow out. Perhaps it was because by then, I was able to comb and brush my own hair. By the time I was 11, my hair was way past my shoulders and stick straight. Then one day, Mom took me to get my hair cut. We were living in the U.S. by that time. Again, it was at a lady's house that did hair out of her home.

On the way there, I asked Mom where we were going. She told me that she was going to have my hair cut. I thought that I was just going to get a trim so didn't think much of it. As I sat in the chair though, I kept seeing long pieces of cut hair fall to the floor. There were no mirrors so I couldn't see what the lady was doing. Next thing you know, my hair had been cut really short. It wasn't even a bob cut that was past my ears, it was like a man's. I was devastated. It took me several years to grow out my hair and then all of a sudden, without asking me, without warning me, Mom has my hair cut really short. The style back then was longer hair, with side layers that were feathered back, after the actress Farrah Fawcett. Even if the style wasn't long, I had wanted to grow my hair out because Mom kept cutting and curling it when I was younger. Yet now I have extra short hair. Why? Was that some form of punishment and for what? While the lady was cutting my hair, Mom had left for a while. When the hairdresser was finished, she handed me the mirror and asked what I thought. I despondently replied, "I look like a boy."

The lady shook her head and said, "Nooo, you don't look like a boy. You look nice."

When I went to school, everyone said they didn't recognize me. One kid said, "Well, I liked your hair the other way. But I guess I'll just have to get used to you looking like this." Even though I received a few compliments, I was still in shock and self conscious about my hair. It was about that time too, when my fingernails began to really grow long. That was the one thing that I did inherit from my mother. She had the ability to grow her nails long naturally and would often receive compliments about them. When Mom noticed that my nails were getting longer, she would tell me angrily, "You need cut your nails. Who say you can have long nails like that?!"

I was perplexed. I wasn't growing them out on purpose. It's just what my nails did. Soon, some of her friends began to notice my nails and hands as well, commenting that I could be a hand model. Mom would just smile because she knew that was the one thing I inherited from her.

**Black and White Memories**

Many people don't remember their childhood experiences before the age of four. But I recall many of those childhood experiences quite vividly, although most of those memories are in black in white with a few exceptions. Mom worked in Nha

Trang, which is approximately 200 miles from Saigon, and cleaned houses. I remember living in Saigon with my grandmother who took care of my older brother Luc and me while Mom worked in Nha Trang. However, I also remember living with Mom in Nha Trang after she married Dad. It was common in the Vietnamese culture for the grandparents to take care of the grandchildren while the parents found work and sent money home. It was and still is common to travel by airplane between the two cities. So at an early age, I was shuffled back and forth via airplane between the two cities several times before the age of four. Little did I know that that was only the beginning of many more moves from one place of residency to another throughout my life. I believe having this early experience on airplanes is what fostered my love for travel and instilled the lack of fear in me for air travel.

While living with my grandmother, Luc had already begun to show signs of being a bully. I remember my grandmother giving us soup to eat out of bright colored plastic bowls. We would sit on the concrete front porch steps with the front door open. After Luc would quickly finish eating his soup, he would take my bowl of soup and eat mine. I would run off crying to my grandmother to tell her what Luc had done, but there would be no words of comfort or turning of her head to even acknowledge I was there. She would remain focused on doing the house work and never made any attempt to discipline Luc. She had better things to do and there was no time for affection or words of encouragement. Besides, Luc was the eldest and a boy. Boys were considered superior to girls. Also, the younger siblings were subservient to their elder siblings, especially if the elder sibling was a boy.

I didn't realize then, just how hard my grandmother worked. I only remember her as being cold, distant, and unemotional.

Interestingly, Mom would tell me that my grandmother loved me very much. I wondered how that could be because I didn't feel it from her. Perhaps it was because she had to work hard and still lived in poverty like many other Vietnamese people during those times. Also, having raised five children and seeing two of her sons die one by one in the war, may have caused her to become hardened and detached as well. Even as I lay sleeping in the same bed as my grandmother, there were never any feelings of warmth or love. I would usually lay by her legs since Luc was sleeping on the same bed.

Because many people were poor, they would often give away their outgrown children's clothes to other families. Mom relayed stories of me seeing a girl in the neighborhood who had a dress that used to belong to me. Mom would chuckle as she recalled how I would go up to the little girl and grab her by the dress and exclaim, "That's my dress!"

Another vivid memory was when I was about three. I had walked over to my next door neighbor's house to see a little girl friend of mine and as I walked across the front yard, I could see their dog, barking and lunging towards me. The dog was medium sized with wavy beige fur, probably just a mutt. However, it could only go so far because it had been tied to a post by a long chain. Despite the ferocious barking and aggressive behavior, I wasn't afraid of the dog. I wanted to see my friend. I thought I could either out run the dog or the dog wouldn't be able to reach me. I was wrong. As I ran for the front door, the mutt lunged towards me and bit me on the outer side of my left thigh. Although I don't recall screaming, that's what I must have done, since several neighbors came running to my aide. The owner of the dog began yelling at the dog and beating it with a broom while other neighbors applied moistened leaves, perhaps an herbal paste, on my wound. As I heard the dog howling, I felt bad for it, more so than I did for myself. The bite left a scar on my leg for many years. After a while though, the scar faded. Yet, despite that experience, I never developed a fear of dogs.

# 2 Children Should Be Seen and Not Heard

I was four and James was two when we moved to Clark Air Base located on the island of Luzon, the largest island in the Philippines. Out of the three of us, Luc, James, and me, only James and I were able to move to the Philippines with my parents. Clark Air Base was the largest American base overseas, covering about 14 miles in diameter. It was located approximately nine miles east of Mount Pinatubo, which I recall seeing growing up. Mount Pinatubo was the most perfect shaped volcano I'd ever seen. When I heard on the news in 1991 that Mt. Pinatubo had erupted and demolished Clark Air Base nearby, it made me sad. I had wanted to go back someday to visit the place where I spent most of my younger childhood days.

My grandmother and oldest brother Luc, who was six, could not come with us due to red tape. I was later told that because Luc was older, he couldn't get a clearance to come with us. Many years later, I learned that because he was a male and from a different father, this also prevented him from getting approved to come with us. I was four and didn't think much of it at the time. When we landed in Clark Air Base and then made our way off base to our new home, our maid Rosita greeted us outside in front of our new home. She was so excited to see us and kneeled down with her arms wide open to hug James, commenting and raving on how cute he was. Then, when she looked over at me, I could see her enthusiasm and excitement diminish. It was as if she said, "Oh, you're his sister?" As she led us into the house, I couldn't help but feel left out and—not cute.

One day, after we had been in our new home for about a week, Dad came home with a big box that was almost as tall as he was. As James and I sat with anticipation on the concrete patio floor, we watched him open the box and then one by one, he pulled out all kinds of toys, stuffed animals, Barbie dolls for me, soldiers for James, etc. The first two toys that Dad pulled out was a stuffed monkey, which he gave to me and a stuffed Koala Bear, which he gave to James. James and I believed that the Koala Bear's claws were from real Koala Bears.

We also got our own tricycles. Mine was red and James's was lime green. One day, when trying to adjust the seat on my bike, which had somehow gotten off alignment and sat crooked on the top tube frame, I severely cut my right ring finger. I was holding the rear side of the seat bottom with my right hand, my palm facing up and with my fingers curled and gripping the metal seat. As I pulled the seat to align with the frame, my fingers got caught between the seat and the frame. The metal edge of the seat cut the top portion of my right ring finger, close to where the first joint was located. Immediately, blood squirted out and I felt a sharp pain. The blood spattered onto my shirt but I didn't scream, yell or cry. I guess I was in a little bit of a shock so I just remained calm and I tried to move the seat with my left hand but it wouldn't move.

James looked over at me and asked, "What happened?"

"My fingers are stuck. Go get Rosita," I implored.

James ran to the house to get Rosita and she rushed out to see what had happened. She moved the seat to release my hand and immediately applied pressure. The piece of flesh that was cut from my finger was almost severed off but fortunately, Rosita took me to a medical clinic where they were able to wrap up the finger and keep it intact. I remember walking to the clinic because Rosita didn't have a car. The medical staff had wrapped a wooden stick that aligned with my finger to keep me from bending it. After my finger healed, it left a bulging oval scar that I still have till this day.

One day, James and I went outside to ride our tricycles but we couldn't find James's tricycle. We looked everywhere but it was gone. We went back into the house and told Mom and Dad that we couldn't find his tricycle. They told us that someone must have stolen it. Since there were no fences around the homes in the area to keep people from coming up to the house, that certainly was possible. Also, there was no need to bring in the tricycles close to the house since it was a pretty safe neighborhood. So the thought never occurred to us that someone would actually do such a mean thing. I felt bad for James that he no longer had his tricycle.

A few days later, I asked my parents if they were going to get another tricycle for James. They said they were planning to but didn't want to tell him about it. What actually occurred was that they had given his tricycle to one of their friend's son but they didn't want James to get upset so they thought it would be easier to make him think someone had stolen it. While I understood that my parents didn't want James to get upset about them giving his bike away, I didn't quite understand why they had to make up a story that wasn't true. It made me wonder if James really would have gotten upset, knowing that his bike was going to another kid, and that he was going to get a new one. It wasn't long though before James got a new bike, one that he could grow into.

Out of all my brothers, James and I were the closest growing up. In the first house we lived in, which was off base, he and I had to share rooms. At night, we would build fortresses on our beds with pillows blocking us in to keep the monsters from getting to us. We imagined tigers and other wild beasts that were lurking under our beds and hiding in the closets.

However, the only real beasts that roamed around the houses in the Philippines were the house gecko. The ones we saw would range from five to eight inches, including their tails and were grayish tan in color. They usually crawled high on the walls and ceilings and on the rare occasion we could reach and actually grab a hold of them, usually by their tails, they would release their tails and run off. That was their way of ensuring their survival because later they would just regenerate another tail. In the mean time, we would be left holding a wiggling tail, which would freak us out.

During the day, Dad would be working and because Mom now had a house maid, she often wouldn't be home. So Rosita would take James and me with her when my parents weren't home. We would walk all over the place and go to different markets. The town and area we lived in was rural, with very few paved roads or sidewalks. We would follow Rosita on dirt roads and trails. There were always lots of green tropical plants and vegetation around us. She would take us to the open markets where we could get a fresh young coconut from a street vendor who had a wheeled cart full of coconuts. The vendor would chop off just the right amount of the coconut skin, husk and skull to where you could see the soft white coconut flesh. Then he would insert a straw through the hole he had made so we could drink the coconut water. It was very refreshing since it was typically scorching hot.

Another refreshing food we would eat while walking around in the open market was halo-halo, which means mix-mix. There are many varieties of this cold and sweet dessert but the one I remember was served in a tall glass. It was made with avocado that was blended with sweetened evaporated milk. Then maize (corn), kidney beans, tapioca, and a variety of fruits, such as cubed mango, would be added along with crushed ice. You would eat the halo-halo with a spoon. The avocado, which tasted sweet in this desert, was the only way I had eaten avocado before so when I moved to the U.S. and ate guacamole for the first time, I didn't like it. At least not at first. Then eventually I acquired a taste for it.

We also began eating more American foods. I don't recall who cooked, whether it was Dad or Rosita, but the first time I ate mashed potatoes, I almost gagged. Dad was sitting next to me and I told him that I didn't like them. I don't know if I had taken too big of a bite or just wasn't used to the texture. Dad told me to eat it anyway. We always had to eat everything off our plates. Throughout the years Dad would say, "Do you know how many kids are starving in China? Eat your food!" And we would comply. We were not allowed to leave anything on our plates and we had to sit at the table until we finished eating everything.

One time, Rosita took us to an area that was close to a cliff. While she was talking to someone, James and I walked to the ledge to get a peek over the edge. We were so high from the valley below, perhaps several hundred feet that it made me dizzy. I had never looked down a cliff before. I felt a pulling sensation coming from the deep valley below, drawing me closer and closer to the edge. My legs began to move, and then all of a sudden, I felt Rosita's hand pulling me back.

"Come on. Let's go," she said.

Rosita held my hand and had me walk on one side of her, and held James' hand as he walked on the other side of her. I wondered if she knew about the pulling sensation that we felt and that's why she kept holding our hands.

I asked James excitedly, "Did you feel that?"

He replied, "Yes."

"Did it feel like it was pulling you?"

"Yeah, it did!"

I don't know if it was the pull of gravity but it felt strange. Along the way home, we would see other children, playing and running near the edge. We walked by a boulder that laid close to the edge of the cliff and saw a little boy sitting on the boulder. James and I stared at him. The other kids were obviously accustomed to being close to the edge since apparently the pull had no effect on them.

Another time Rosita took us off base, there was a parade going on. This wasn't your ordinary happy and cheerful parade. It was during Holy Week, the Easter tradition of crucifixion and self flogging in a procession was taking place. As James and I peeked through the crowd of people to see what was happening, we saw adult Filipino men walking on their knees in the streets and flogging themselves on the back with whips made of bamboo. We saw other men being carried on a cross by their peers. It was a very gruesome sight and we didn't understand why these men were torturing themselves. We asked Rosita why they were doing these things but whatever explanation she gave still didn't make sense to us. That was the first and only time we saw anything like that.

## Imagined Discomfort

Prior to living in the Philippines, I had never been to the dentist. Since Dad was in the Air Force and had good bene-fits, he was able to take me to see the dentist. The first time I went, I was terrified. The dentist had determined that my gums were too small for all my adult teeth that would be coming in. They gave me Novocain and of course the injection hurt. Despite how numb I felt after the injection, I was still afraid of what was about to happen. When the dentist came in to pull two of my teeth, I began to scream. He called for reinforcements and had two dental assistants come in to hold me down. I didn't know at the time why I reacted the way I did because I didn't recall feeling any pain during the extraction. But I was only five and was very frightened. Afterwards, with my mouth full of gauze and while walking down the dental office hall with Dad, I thought how silly I was for reacting the way I did, putting up such a fuss when I didn't feel a thing except the pinch from the Novocain shot. I was sorry for the trouble that I had caused and promised myself that I wouldn't react that way again.

It's a good thing I realized that I didn't feel any pain because I had to have another dental appointment to extract more teeth. This time, they put a warm, damp cloth over my eyes, asked if I was doing okay, to which I affirmed I was, and pulled out five more of my baby teeth. They had brought in two dental assistants but this time, they only needed one. Apparently, they remembered my previous dramatic reaction. Afterwards, when they showed me how my teeth looked, I was astonished to see the pointed shapes of the teeth, which were the roots. I quickly learned that things aren't always as bad as we imagine them to be and things don't always appear the way we think they do.

When we first moved to the Philippines, I didn't realize that I had been speaking in Vietnamese. Gradually, I had completely forgotten that Vietnamese was my first language. The transition from Vietnamese to English was so smooth that in my mind I had always just spoken one language. I do recall James and me calling Dad "Ba", which is "father" in Vietnamese. That was okay while we were living in Vietnam but now that we had moved to the Philippines and were living on an American military base which was predominately occupied by Americans who spoke English, Dad wanted to be called "dad". "Why don't you just call me dad from now on?" he asked. From that point on, we did.

When I was a teenager, I asked Mom why she didn't keep speaking to James and me in Vietnamese. She explained that she had a friend who had a little girl that didn't know how to speak English. The little girl was in class one day and she had to go pee but she didn't know how to tell the teacher that in English. The teacher, not knowing what the little girl wanted, refused to let her go to the bathroom and the child ended up peeing in her pants. Then the teacher became very angry with the little girl.

Mom didn't want that to happen to me so she wanted me and James to learn English as quickly as possible. She didn't think we could learn both. When I heard that explanation, I understood why Mom stopped talking to me and James in Vietnamese but I was saddened that she didn't know that children are like sponges and can learn multiple languages at the same time.

Interestingly, as an adult and living in the U.S., I would meet other Asian Americans and some Mexican Americans who didn't speak their native language. That's because during the 70's it was not popular for minority or ethnic parents to teach their children to speak in their native language because they wanted their children to become more "American". At least that's how it was in the smaller rural communities. It was so fascinating to me to learn that there were others who were like me, who were non-Caucasian Americans but who could only speak English.

Gradually, the influx of more foreigners made that trend disappear. Because the population of newer minorities or ethnic groups increased, it made it more comfortable for them to speak with each other and their children in their native language. There was a community of their own culture or race that they could connect with so they didn't feel they needed to have their children speak only English.

One day when I was five, my parents told me that we were going to Guam for a vacation. It was really so I could get my U.S. Citizenship. That's why James couldn't go with us. I didn't understand why and it made me feel sad to leave him behind, even though he would be cared for by our maid. I remember seeing him watching us leave and crying through the front screen door as we were driving away because he couldn't come with us.

We were in Guam for about a week but my strongest memory of being there was when we went to the beach. At first I was a bit hesitant about getting into the water since I had never been on a beach before, but as an adult friend of my parents coaxed me to get in, I decided to go ahead and test the waters. It wasn't long before I was having a good time playing and swimming in the water and feeling the surge and pull of the waves rolling in then out.

Suddenly, a huge and powerful wave swept in and pulled me into its grip. I could feel the mix of sand and water all around me as I was being pulled upward by the force of the wave. I held my breath for as long as I could and swam as hard as I could to reach the surface, but I couldn't find it. After what seemed like a very long time, the wave finally released its grip on me and violently dropped me onto the sandy shore. As soon as my head came out of the water I gasped for air. I immediately thought, *I will never swim so far out and deep into the ocean again, especially if the waves appear to be big and powerful. The ocean is not one to be reckoned with and I am fortunate I didn't drown.*

When I was able to stand and walk out of the water, there was no one around to see if I was okay. Nobody had seen me get pulled in by the giant and mighty wave and there was nobody I could tell. I eventually found the picnic table where my parents and their friends were but I was too shy to say anything or tell them about the powerful wave that almost took my life. I recall them asking me if I had fun, to which I sheepishly replied, "Yes". After the warm tropical air had dried my skin and lime green swim suit, I noticed that there was sand inside my swim suit. I wondered how all this sand got inside. Ahh, it was from the powerful waves.

Later that evening, my parents and I went over to their friends' house for dinner. All I remember was that one of the older kids took me into their room and read a book to me while we were lying on the bed. She had me lay next to her, with my head resting on one of her arms as she held the book up for me to see. That was the first time anyone had read a book to me or lay next to me in bed that way. Although I slept in the same bed as my grandmother, it wasn't the same. She didn't hold me close to her like this older girl did. It felt strange but I just went along with it. I must have been exhausted because it didn't take long for me to fall asleep. When I awoke, it was the next morning and I was still in the same room, in the same bed, and in the same clothes. The mother offered me a warm washcloth to freshen up and wipe my face. Those days, I didn't talk much. "Would you like a wash cloth?" I nodded my head. *Wow! No one has ever offered me a warm washcloth before.* Soon though, my parents came to pick me up. I really didn't want to go with them. I wanted to stay with the family to see what other new and different things I could learn and experience from them.

I vaguely recall being in the USCIS office where my picture was taken to get my U.S. Citizenship. While my parents and I were sitting in the waiting area to be called up next, an American Caucasian man dressed in a military uniform who was possibly in his 20's or 30's walked over to me and then knelt down to my level. He looked at me with his sparkling blue eyes and with a smile said, "You are going to be very cute when you grow up." I had no idea why he said that and why he seemed to like me. Being told I was cute wasn't something I heard very often, so I just looked at him without saying a word.

On the airplane going back home to the Philippines, I told my parents I wanted to bring home a gift for James. So I saved the unopened miniature box of Frosted Flakes that had Tony the Tiger on it and a box of Cracker Jax popcorn with a toy inside the box to give to him. When we arrived back at our house, James was elated to see us. I gave him the little box of Frosted Flakes and the box of Cracker Jax which made him very happy.

## Letting the Music Die

When we lived in the first house on base, I loved to sing and would often still sing Christmas carols around the house even when Christmas was over. One day in January, I was singing "Jingle Bells". Dad was in the kitchen and heard me singing. He turned to me and said in a condescending tone, "Why are you still singing that? Christmas is over." Apparently, my singing was annoying to him. I obviously loved to sing but sensed how irritated and annoyed he was. So I never sang around the house again, especially not in front of Dad. Just that one comment was enough for me to let the music in me die. I don't know why I took things so seriously. I wished I had more courage and confidence but I didn't. I was like a blade of grass growing on rocky ground. With one slight breeze my roots would give way and I would be blown away.

My parents were very strict with us growing up and didn't allow us to curse or even call each other stupid. During the early days, it was just me and James. If one of us did call each other stupid, we would tell our parents and the one who did the name calling would be readily reprimanded verbally. Also, if I was to say or do something that Mom didn't like, I would get a quick slap in the face without warning. It seemed like she was easily provoked and got angry with only the slightest provocation. One time, she slapped me so hard on the face that I ended up getting a bloody nose. I didn't know what I did but without warning, she would slap me. Perhaps she just wanted me to be quiet and not talk. When I noticed that I had a bloody nose, I didn't know what to do. Mom had walked away so the maid was left to help stop the bleeding. I remember Rosita giving me a paper towel to hold up to my nose and telling me to pinch the bridge of my nose and lean my head back. After that, I learned to stay away from Mom because I just didn't know what I would do that would set her off so easily.

We also had to say "thank you" or "please" and when it came to addressing adults, we had to say "Mr." or "Mrs." so-and-so even though sometimes the adult would want us to call them by their first name. Then, when it came to adult friends of the family, we had to call them uncle so-and-so or auntie so-and-so out of respect.

We also weren't given a lot of sweets, candy or sodas to eat or drink. Every now and then, we were allowed to have a Ho Ho or a Ding Dong chocolate cake as a treat but that was on rare occasions. Every time Mom or Dad said Ding Dong, James and I would giggle. Also, sodas were not a common staple in our house. The only time James and I were able to have a soda was when we went off base. While Mom was making sales of items she purchased at the BX to selects vendors in the Market Place, which was also called the "Black Market", Dad would take me and James to a bar. Dad would have a beer while James would have an orange soda, and I would get a Pepsi. We always got the same thing every time we sat at the bar, waiting for Mom to sell items, mostly cigarettes, in the Black Market.

Sometimes, Mom would just take me and James to sell things under the Black Market, either by herself or with a friend, and without Dad. During those times, while we were crossing the gate and check points for leaving and entering the base, she would tell me and James to stand up in the car. I never understood why she told us to do that. We seldom had to stop for questioning and often times would drive right through the check points.

# 3 My Favorite Teacher and Hero

It didn't take long before Dad enrolled me into preschool. I remember riding the bus through the tropical landscape and watching the other kids. I recall staring at one little girl who had loops of thread in her ear lobes. She'd recently had her ears pierced. The loops of thread and her piercing holes were red from the stain of Mercurochrome™, which was used as an antiseptic for cuts and scrapes.

One of the few things I remember about first grade was this little boy who kept lifting my dress up. I have one recollection where he whispered to me and told me to come with him. Then he would lead me behind a book-shelf in the classroom where no one could see us and lift up my dress. It would make me so angry when he did that. Mom told me later that I would come home from school crying because this little boy was constantly lifting my dress up. However, Mom kept making me wear dresses throughout grade school. It wasn't until I reached about fifth grade that I was allowed to wear pants. After that, I never wore dresses to school again since I had developed a loathing of them.

In second grade, I recall having an art period where we would get to draw. I actually drew quite well so that the other kids asked me to draw for them. I realized when the other kids asked me to draw for them, that I had natural talent. I thought about growing up to be an artist but then immediately dismissed that notion and told myself that I'd never be able to make a living doing art. Where did I get that from? My parents never told me I couldn't draw or wasn't good at art since I hadn't taken any art home yet from school. How would they know? As an adult, I was perplexed as to where that thought had come from. Did I hear it from someone else?

Then, when I was in the seventh grade, I had an art class and did so well in it that the Art Teacher gave me some pictures to sketch and draw that he didn't give to the other students. He obviously noticed my natural talent as well. They were pictures of nude women and other figures. I was 11 and wasn't comfortable drawing the pictures of the nude women. When a couple of classmates asked me what I was drawing, I showed them. I also mentioned to one of the girls that I wasn't comfortable drawing pictures of the nude women. Although I didn't ask her to, she went and told the teacher. I couldn't understand why she did that and became irritated with her. I could have told the teacher myself.

The teacher then came over to my desk and said, "I caught you!" I asked a little startle, "What?" I thought I was in trouble for not wanting to draw the pictures of nude women. He said, "You're chewing gum in class and you're not supposed to chew gum." I was relieved. I said, "Oh, okay," and took the gum out of my mouth. Then he said, "I understand you don't feel comfortable drawing some of these pictures. That's okay. You don't have to draw them. I will give you some other things to draw." So I agreed to draw the other pictures he gave me. Surprisingly, I got a "B" in the class. I didn't understand why when I thought I had done so well and that the teacher saw potential in me. The only reason I could think of why I didn't get an "A" was because I didn't want to draw the nude pictures, which I didn't feel was very fair of him. But I didn't have the courage to talk to him about it so I just accepted the "B".

Other than that, art was an easy subject for me. One of my favorite figures to draw with a protractor was the evenly-spaced overlapping circles that formed into a flower. I didn't know it at the time but I was drawing the Flower of Life. I don't know how I came to draw them since nobody ever showed me how to draw them, and I don't remember seeing them anywhere at home or any other place in school. But I somehow figured out that if you kept overlapping the circles, you could keep going on and on with the same pattern and you would get a page full of flowers. It was just something that came natural for me to draw and I would draw them while the Art Teacher was lecturing.

Even in high school, any art class I took, I easily got A's. When I heard that some kids struggled with it, I couldn't understand why. Even though it came easy for me and I knew I had potential, I still remember having that thought in second grade that I couldn't make a living out of it and so I never pursued my artistic abilities.

## No Mother-Daughter Bond

Despite not getting affection or feeling loved by Mom, living in the Philippines was the closest to having a normal childhood as any child could. My brother James and I got to ride our bikes all over the base. During those times and perhaps living on an American base the level of crime was quite low. James and I rarely watched TV and didn't watch the news if we did. Usually one of the maids would have a Filipino show on. We really didn't listen to music much either because we were always outside playing. So we never thought or had any fear of something bad happening to us. As strict as our parents were, it was surprising that we were able to go almost anywhere we wanted on our bikes.

When we finally moved on base, the first house we lived in was located on a cul-de-sac. It was on that cul-de-sac where I first learned to ride a bike. It was a girly bike with a pink banana seat and a white plastic weaved basket in front of the steering bars. The basket also had plastic flowers in front of it. Some of the other kids in the cul-de-sac who had already learned to ride their bikes and who had been riding for a while told me that I really didn't know how to ride a bike until I was able ride up and down the sidewalk curb. Fortunately the edges of the curb weren't exactly 90 degree angles and were slanted so I was able to maneuver up and down the side walks like they did. So now, I *really* knew how to ride a bike.

Then for some reason, my parents decided to move from living in a house that was located in the circular part of the cul-de-sac to a house on the corner of the same cul-de-sac. That's where I met Melissa, the one who told me a few years later that Dad was not my real Dad. Melissa and I would hang out together while her mom and my mom would visit. After hanging out with her a few times, she told me that we were best friends and I went along with it. We would also play together when her mother would come over and visit with my mother, but often we would just talk or rather, Melissa would talk. She would talk mostly about her mom, how she and her mom didn't get along very well. Melissa felt comfortable talking to me and I mostly listened. I didn't feel warmth or love from Mom either but didn't have the words to express that.

Instead, they were translated into my dreams. I would often dream about Mom leaving me. In the dreams, I would be on my knees begging her not to leave me. I would wake up crying and feeling empty and abandoned. I would ponder why I would have such a dream since Mom was there physically. I knew she wasn't going anywhere. It wasn't until I got older that I realized why I had those dreams. It was because I felt abandoned by her emotionally. It became clear to me that she had already abandoned me emotionally prior to my birth.

In school I learned about mothers and babies bonding and how important it was for that to take place. I also learned how important it was for babies to feel loved by their mothers and to be held by them or at least by someone else. Without being held or shown love, the babies would eventually die. After learning that concept, I knew instantly that Mom and I didn't have that bond. It wasn't there when I was an infant and it wasn't there as I was growing up. I wondered how I had survived. I came to realize that she just wasn't capable of showing love or affection to me because of her resentment towards her first husband, my biological father.

So because I never felt I was loved by Mom, I turned to Dad. During those years, life was good and there was less stress. Dad had a good job and was able to provide for his family. He was the more stable and affectionate one. Sometimes, he would tickle me until I couldn't stand it anymore.

One night, as he was tucking me into bed, I asked him, "Daddy, do you love me?" He replied, "Of course I love you. Why do you ask?" Then he gave me a kiss on the forehead and pulled the sheets over me. I didn't say anything back because I didn't know how to tell him that I didn't feel loved by Mom. Even though I knew he wasn't my biological father, I knew that he loved me. I never felt that he treated me any different than my brother, at least not during those days, and I knew that he would always be there for me.

When I was about seven, I asked Mom where I had come from. We were living in the second house on base. This question must have been on my mind for quite some time since I was bold enough to ask her that while she had a friend over visiting. They were seated at our dining room table when I approached her. She chuckled and said, "I found you in a garbage can."

That was the Vietnamese way, so I was told many years later, but I didn't know that. I was a very sensitive kid and couldn't understand why Mom would say that. Other times, when she was angry at me, she would tell me that when I die, I would go to Hell. I began to worry about that so I would go to Dad and say, "Dad, when I grow up and I become a good girl, will I still go to Hell?" Dad replied, "No, if you became a good girl, then you won't go to Hell." I was relieved. At least there was some hope for me.

## Tropical Living

One of the great things about living in the Philippines was the delicious tropical fruits. Sometimes there were fruit trees in the neighborhood where we could just go up to them and pick the fruits. A few cul-de-sacs down, there was a tall star apple tree. The first time I saw the tree, there were a few people around it, picking the fruit from off the ground and off the tree. I asked someone about the fruit, which was round shaped, about four inches in diameter and had thick and purple leathery skin. When the fruit is cut in half through the middle and transversely, the seed cells radiated from the center to look like an asterisks or star, hence the name. The skin and seeds of the fruit are not eaten but the flesh is very delicious.

There was one particular house in the neighborhood that had a guava tree in the front yard. Melissa and I loved eating guavas, with its green skin and pink seedy and soft flesh, so we would climb the neighbor's guava tree and picked some of the delicious fruit. One day a lady peeped out the front window and yelled at us to get off her tree, causing us to run off. The lady had startled and scared us. However, that didn't keep us from returning. We just couldn't resist going back to get more guavas but we were extra cautious and made sure we were very quiet. It seemed that the owners must have been day sleepers because the blinds were always closed.

There was also a rambutan tree in the neighborhood, whose fruit has a hairy and soft red rubbery outer skin, but inside the flesh is white and sweet. Other fruits I've eaten while living in the Philippines were the breadfruit, durian, jackfruit, with its aromatic flesh, lychee, papaya, mango, pummelo, which looked like a giant grapefruit, starfruit, which was different than the star apple, soursop, sugarapple and tamarind. There were also a variety of bananas, including baby bananas and plantains. It never occurred to me that when we moved to the U.S., we would not have those fruits available to eat. Every now and then, Mom would find some of the fruits in an Asian market but that rarely occurred.

One early morning, neighborhood kids came to our home and asked James and I to join them in playing "follow the leader". Our parents were still asleep and we didn't think to ask for their permission. It just sounded like so much fun so there we were, roaming the neighborhood, in the light tropical mist, walking down into empty concrete water ditches and then back out again, climbing up trees, climbing over and on fences, jumping off roofs of houses. I don't know how we managed to jump from that high off the ground and not break any bones. There was no fear. We just followed our fearless leader, who was one of the older kids in the neighborhood.

I believe though that this is when I may have developed a fear of heights or as they say nowadays, fear of falling. If it wasn't developed then by jumping off of the roofs of houses, it may have been when I fell while swinging in a tire that was tied to a tree a few years later. This tree was behind the third house we lived in on base. You had to climb a ladder to get up the tree, then someone from the ground would bring you the tire. You would then get into the tire and jump from the tree while sitting inside the tire. One day though, the rope that was tide from a tree branch and to the tire broke and I fell while still sitting inside the tire. I hit the ground with a heavy thud. Because it happened so fast, I was stunned for a few seconds and just sat there trying to get my bearings.

By the time the older kids brought us back home, our parents met us at the front door, demanding to know where we had been. They looked at the other kids as we explained to them that we had been playing "follow the leader". While James and I expected to get a whipping for leaving the house without permission, we were both surprised that our parents had let us off with just a warning to never do that again.

I was about seven when Dad enrolled James and me in Judo classes. After a while though, I became bored with the classes. There was an American Food kiosk near the gym where the Judo classes were held. One day, I talked James into ditching Judo class. The plan was to tell our instructor that I had a headache and that I couldn't attend class that day. I recall standing outside the gym, telling my instructor that I had a headache as I held my hand to my forehead. The instructor let us both off since I was the older sister and was responsible for him so if I had to go home, then he would have to come with me. Instead of going home though, we headed for the hamburger kiosk and sat on the concrete floor on the side that faced away the gym, so that no one from class could see us. We rarely ever had money with us but that day, we had some change and so I got myself a Pepsi and James got an orange soda, our usual soda of choice.

However, that was the first and last time we ditched Judo classes. Later, I felt bad for lying to the instructor and to Dad. We continued to go until I reached yellow belt, which was the second level after white. I recall beating a younger boy in my first yellow belt competition. We were about the same size and that's why our Judo instructor had us matched up for competition. Afterwards, the younger boy cried and his older brother was there to console him. As they were putting their shoes on, I went over to the where they were sitting and asked if the younger boy was okay. His older brother replied, "Yeah, he'll be okay." However, I could tell that the older brother felt bad for his little brother and I felt bad that I had made the boy cry too. I received a quarter for winning that competition. I remember seeing our Judo instructor walking around with a clear plastic bag of quarters that he gave to the winners of a competition.

My brother James and I would usually get a ride from Dad to Judo class or we would ride our bikes. One day though, James didn't come and Dad had dropped me off. After the class was over, one of the older kids in the class asked me how I was getting home. I noticed that she was a purple belt. I said that Dad had dropped me off and that I guess I could walk. Back then, there were no cell phones and I don't even think I knew how to use a phone if they did have one. Talking on the phone just wasn't something I ever did. So this older girl who rode her bike to class offered to give me a ride home, after she found out where I lived. At first I told her that I would be okay because I was just too shy to let her give me a ride. Besides, where could I sit on her bike since she didn't have a banana seat? But she kept insisting and said I could sit on the handle bars. I guess I was little and light enough for her to do that. So she helped me get up on the handlebars and we rode home that way.

When we reached the driveway where I lived, Dad was just coming out of the house. I guess he saw us through the kitchen window as we were approaching the house. The girl helped me get off the bike and I told her good-bye. As I walked up to Dad, he asked me, "Did you tell her thank you?" I was so shy and surprised by the whole experience of someone else taking care of me other than my parents and the maid that I had forgotten. I also wasn't used to being with kids that much older than me. So I walked back to the girl and quietly said, "Thank you for the ride." She said, "You're welcome," and then she rode off. After that, I never saw her again. I guess I remembered that experience because I felt something from that older girl. I felt her confidence and her desire to want to protect me.

During those years, I was quite the tomboy. It seemed that when I turned ten, I suddenly turned into a girl. I don't know if that had to do with the big change in our lives, the change brought on by moving to the U.S. or something else. However, before the age of ten and while living in the Philippines, I did things I would never do again. Things like catching praying mantises by grasping them from the back of their necks and sticking them into jars. We would punch holes in the lids of the jars with a knife so they had air to breathe and then fed them tiny moths. Sometimes we would put little sticks and leaves in the jars so the praying mantis would have something to climb on. Then my brother James and I would get up early in the morning, while there was still dew on the grass, to catch the tiny moths that would fly low to the ground. These tiny moths would land on the small, white flowers that grew in the grass. I believe the moths would fly around and pollinate these small flowers. So we would catch these tiny moths with our hands and collect them in a plastic bag. Then we would insert them through the slits in the lids of the jars to feed the praying mantis. We would watch the praying mantises catch the moths and eat them.

My brother James and I would also pick up big black beetles and tie a string to one of their legs and then spin them around in the air. This way, we could hear them buzz. Then the grasshoppers didn't stand a chance with us either. We would pick those up, held them by their antlers and legs and then pop their heads off. And finally, the bees were caught with a plastic sandwich bag. When we saw a bee land on a flower, we would enclose the flower with the sandwich bag, hold the flower by the stem, and then break or pop off the flower from the stem so that we would have the flower and the bee in the plastic bag. A couple of times though, I got stung by the bee. Looking back at all those things I had done with insects as a child makes me wonder how I became so fearful and disgusted with them later. I wouldn't dream of doing those things today and just the thought of them would give me tingles and a prickly feeling all over my body.

In third grade, I learned about Bloody Mary. No, it wasn't the drink I had learned about. It was the story the kids would relate about a folklore character named Bloody Mary. They said that if you stood in front of a mirror and chanted her name out loud three times, she would appear. That story got me so scared that one night, I couldn't go to sleep. I was crying and told my parent that I didn't want to sleep in my room because I was afraid Bloody Mary was going to get me. My parents had no idea what I was talking about. They kept saying that it wasn't real but the kids at school had me convinced. So instead of sleeping in my room, my parents said I could sleep on the couch in the living room. Somehow, I was able to fall asleep. The next morning, I woke up and was so surprised that I was still alive. What a relief! I guess the kids at school weren't telling the truth after all. So I never believed in Bloody Mary again.

However, I did come to believe in the Tooth Fairy. When James began to have his baby teeth fall out, my parents told him to put his teeth under his pillow. One night, Mom was sitting in the living room crocheting and Dad was taking a shower. James went into his room to check under his pillow. He discovered that in his tooth's place was a silver dollar. He was ecstatic and I was excited for him. When Dad came out of the shower, we told him excitedly about the Tooth Fairy putting a silver dollar under James's pillow.

"Is that right?" Dad asked.

"Yes, the silver dollar wasn't there before and now it is!" we told him.

Then, I got to thinking. Wow, I had my baby teeth pulled and I've had my baby teeth fall out. How come my parents never told me to put my teeth under the pillow? So I asked them about that.

"Okay, you can put your tooth under your pillow next time you have one fall out."

"Okay," I said excitedly.

So the next time I lost a baby tooth, I put my tooth under my pillow, expecting to get a silver dollar. But instead, I received a couple of quarters. Wow, something doesn't seem right. Was it because I was older or because I was a girl? I was confused.

As time went on, James and I continued to believe in the Tooth Fairy. We no longer believed in Santa Claus because of the stories Dad would tell us about him. We could tell he was making it up. We didn't have a fireplace so Dad would say that Santa had wings and would fly around without the reindeers, but that's not we learned in school so we knew Santa didn't exist. But we were convinced that the Tooth Fairy existed because we didn't see anyone go into the room and put money under the pillow. Later Mom told us that they indeed had put the money under the pillow.

"But you were in the living room and Dad was in the shower," I insisted.

"No, we put there earlier," she replied.

So that explained why James got the silver dollar and I didn't. Even though James was clearly the favorite of the two kids, I still loved him. I didn't feel resentful or jealous of him. I just wished I had looked different. That I was lighter skinned. I don't know why I wished that I had blond hair and blue eyes growing up but I did. It's not like we had any beauty or fashion magazines with American models lying around the house and we didn't watch a lot of television either. Perhaps it was because we lived on an American base that was predominately occupied by Caucasian Americans, so I was still considered a minority. Even in school, there weren't very many Asians. That's just how it was and that's what I was used too.

When I was seven, Mom tried to teach me how to crochet but I couldn't quite grasp the skill so she got frustrated with me and left off from teaching me until I was eight. For some reason, eight was the magic age for me. I learned to crochet and soon I was helping Mom make dining room tablecloths and other decorative cloths for the furniture around the house. It was also at that age I learned how to keep secrets. Mom didn't trust our maid so she told me to keep an eye on her. One day in conversation, I told our maid that Mom told me to keep watch over her. When our maid mentioned that to Mom, Mom became very angry with me and gave me a severe scolding. I remember her stern and angry look as she looked down at me while I was crocheting outside by the car port. After that, I learned the skill of discernment, how to keep secrets, and when to keep my mouth shut.

**For Every One Negative, There Must Be Ten Positives**

For some reason, it seemed I changed schools as often as our family moved houses. That's why I didn't always have the same friends and didn't always have the same teachers. Yet one of my most memorable teachers was when I was in third grade. Mrs. Rittenhouse was a tall lady with short graying hair and big blue eyes. She must have been in her fifties at the time. Mrs. Rittenhouse taught us cursive writing, among other things. I remember practicing one time to write in cursive. We were given letters, words, and sentences to practice writing. There was a line below the example and if it was a letter or word, there was plenty of room to practice, over and over. I recall a student asked how many times we were to practice writing the letter or word. Wow! I hadn't thought about a limiting amount of times to practice the letter or word. I just kept practicing until I filled the line. Then I heard Mrs. Rittenhouse reply with the answer I had already been doing.

"Just keep writing for as long as you want. There's no set number of times you should write the letter or word. You could fill up the line below if you want."

One day, we started an art project. We were to make a puppet out of paper mache. This was an ongoing project and it took us several days to complete. The body of the puppet was made of a piece of fabric that was in the shape of a shirt with two holes on each side for the sleeves. The shirt was glued to the paper mache head and we would stick our hand through the opening of the fabric at the bottom, then stick our thumb out of one side and our ring finger out the other side and then our index and middle fingers into the head. When we finally had the head set, we began painting the face of the puppet. I looked around the classroom and noticed a few of the other kids were painting their puppet's nose red. *So typical* I thought. I decided that I wanted my puppet to be different than everyone else's so I painted my puppet's nose green. After our puppets were finished, I brought mine home. Mom was home and sitting at the dining room table. I didn't see Dad but evidently he was in the kitchen. I was so excited about my puppet so I showed it to Mom. This was the first time I had brought anything home from school.

Immediately Mom said, "What is that?"

"It's a puppet."

"What is puppet?"

"You stick your hand in it and you can make it talk."

"It is ugly! Go throw it away!"

I was devastated. I had been working on this project for several days and was so proud of it. I was also proud that my puppet's head was different than the other kids because mine had a green nose instead of a red one and now Mom tells me to go throw it away? I ran into my room and slammed the door behind me. I was so angry at Mom and hurt for what she said. I threw the puppet into the trash, then knelt by my bed, put my head down on my folded arms and cried.

I could hear Dad scorning Mom, "Why did you say that to her? You're not supposed to say things like that!"

"Well, it ugly," Mom insisted.

"I don't care. You're not supposed to do that!" Dad replied.

Soon, Dad came and opened the bedroom door. I looked up at him, trying to hold back the tears.

"Eden, don't listen to your mother. It's very nice what you made. Don't throw it away. Okay?"

I just nodded my head. He closed the door and I cried even harder. It was too late. The damage was done. I left the puppet in the small trash bin.

The next day, Mrs. Rittenhouse asked us what our parents thought of our puppets. I heard the other kids tell their stories of how proud their parents were of them. My eyes started tearing up. I tried so hard to hold them back but I couldn't. Mrs. Rittenhouse noticed and called me up to her desk. She asked me quietly what was wrong. I almost couldn't talk. As I fought back the tears, I told her in a very low and shaky voice, "My mom thought it was... She thought it was ugly and she told me to throw it away." Mrs. Rittenhouse looked at me for a few seconds with her softly wrinkled face and her big blue eyes, then she held my arm and said, "You tell your mother that you worked very hard on that puppet. Tell her that I told you that you did a great job on it and that your puppet is very pretty. Okay?"

I nodded my head and went back to my seat but I knew that I would not be retrieving the puppet since our maid had already thrown away the trash.

It just seemed so difficult to please Mom. I don't recall her ever giving me a compliment and saying I had done well about anything. When we moved to our third house on base, I would play with some of the kids in the neighborhood but mostly, I would play with my friend next door named Gina who was half Filipino and half Caucasian. When I looked at Gina, I noticed that her nose wasn't like her mother's nose, who was Filipino. Gina was also very slim and tall for her age and her complexion was golden tan but lighter than her mothers. It seemed her skin color was a perfect blend of her mother's and father's. Her hair was also lighter, a medium brown color rather than black or dark brown. I concluded that Gina looked liked like her American Caucasian father. Her younger brother George was shorter and had very dark hair and his facial features were more like his Filipino mother. They were the perfect hereditary pattern that I came to realize later.

On the other hand, James would often play with George. Occasionally, James and George would want to hang out with me and Gina. Sometimes this would bother us and we would tell them to leave us alone and to go play by themselves. Often, Gina and I would play with our Barbie dolls on the front porch of my house. My parents had a rule for James and I to never enter into a neighbor's house without permission and none of the neighbor kids could just come into our house unless we asked for permission to let them come in. So I rarely ever got to go inside Gina's house, even though they were right next door as part of the duplex.

If Gina wasn't around, I would often play on the front porch by myself with my three Barbie dolls and their house. I would somehow find scraps of material to make my Barbie doll clothes. I must have gotten the scraps from leftover fabric that Mom's seamstress would use to make Mom's clothes. I was very proud of the clothes that I made for my Barbie dolls since I would hand sew them together. I figured I was saving my parents money by making the clothes for them. That way, my parents wouldn't have to buy the clothes for them. Plus, my Barbie dolls would have unique clothes that nobody else had. One day, when I was sitting on the front porch with my Barbie doll set, Mom opened the front door and looked down at me and at what I was doing. She had company inside and for some reason decided to open the door to see what I was doing. I don't know what prompted her to open the door. Perhaps she heard me talking to myself. I really wasn't a loud kid. I wasn't allowed to be and had to be careful around Mom because she could unleash her fumes at a moment's notice. As she looked down at me with displeasure, she mentioned something about the clothes I was making for my Barbie dolls. Some type of disapproval, although that wasn't the word that she used. I didn't understand why she had gotten upset. I was just playing by myself and not causing any trouble. I wasn't in the house being noisy or getting in anybody's way. Perhaps the dresses and clothes I made weren't exactly the best tailor made clothing since I had sewn them by hand and nobody had taught me how to sew. I was only nine but figured it out by myself and was actually quite proud of my creations. But I guess in her eyes, they looked like rags. She seemed so upset at what I was doing that if she didn't have company over, I was afraid she would have struck me. Of course, that wouldn't have been anything new. If she didn't want me to play on the front porch, she never said anything about it. So, I continued to play on the front porch with my Barbie doll set by myself or with my neighbor friend Gina.

For the most part, I was a pretty good, obedient and quiet student. I rarely raised attention to myself or caused a disturbance in class. One day though, I did get into a little trouble. It wasn't without the help of another student though. That day, my teacher and the teacher in the class next to us decided to combine our classes together so both classes could watch a film on how heat travels in different types of substances, such as in different cooking utensils. The film showed how heat from a pot would travel faster in a metal cooking utensil than in a wooden cooking utensil.

During the film, I was seated on the floor towards the front of the class. Since the teacher had to squeeze all the students together into one classroom, some students were on the floor like me and some were sitting in desks. I was sitting next to a classmate named Pamela. Pamela was an African American girl who was quite artistic. During that time, Pamela had some paper with her and asked me to draw a bunch of squiggly lines and loops on a piece of paper without picking up my pen. She told me that no matter what I drew, she could turn it into something. So I drew a bunch of squiggly lines and loops and sure enough, she drew a lady out of the abstract shapes of lines and loops that I had drawn. It was really neat to see her creative ability. After the film was over, my teacher got up and started asking questions about the film we saw.

Unfortunately, because we were at the front of the class, my teacher saw us and didn't think that Pamela and I were paying attention so the teacher asked me how the heat traveled in a metal cooking utensil. "I don't know," I replied, because the film didn't explain "how" the heat traveled but that it traveled faster in the metal utensil than the wooden utensil.

"You see, that's why you should have been paying attention," she chided in front of the whole class. She then asked if someone else knew the answer. Another kid answered the question and stated that the heat traveled faster in the metal utensil. I thought, *I was paying attention*, and wanted to tell the teacher that the film didn't explain *how* the heat traveled but decided to let it go. It was enough for me to be singled out in front of the classroom like that and I wasn't used to getting in trouble or getting attention that way at school. I didn't get mad at Pamela though. I just wished that I didn't allow her to distract me from paying attention to the teacher. The teachers were pretty strict. Some more than others and I knew better.

For example, Mr. Peterson, one of my fourth grade teachers, was much stricter than the other teachers. We had to sit at our desks with our hands clasps together on top of our desks. If we had a question or knew the answer to a question, we were to raise our hand and if called upon, stand and ask the question or provide the answer. Mr. Peterson taught history and one of the historical lessons we learned was about World War II, which involved the German Nazis.

One evening, Dad revealed that he was German. I don't recall how the subject came up. Perhaps it was because I told him that I was learning about World War II. My first thought was, *Germans – Nazis. Was he one of those bad Nazis*?

"You're not German. You're an American," I replied.

"No, I'm German."

He couldn't be! Then as I thought about it, I concluded that Dad was a nice man and if he really were a Nazi, he wouldn't be here. No, of course he wasn't a Nazi.

At the same time, I hadn't noticed that he had a slight German accent. When we moved to the U.S. and lived in Merced, some of our neighborhood kid friends told me and James that when we first moved into the neighborhood, they had noticed that Dad had an accent.

We told them, "Our dad doesn't have an accent."

They insisted, "Yes he does."

Then I thought about it. The only accent he could have had was German. He didn't speak Vietnamese because he never had to learn to speak Vietnamese. Since so many Vietnamese people could speak French, Dad was able to get away with speaking French and English while he was there in Vietnam.

Our fifth grade class was having a Christmas exchange party. I told Mom that I needed to bring a gift to school for our Christmas party. Mom forgot about it so I reminded her again, the day before the party. Mom had just come back from the commissary and decided that she didn't want to go out again to get a gift. So she pulled a box of dates out of her bag of groceries. She said I could bring the dates as a gift. I was horrified and began to get very annoyed at her. I told her that it needed to be a toy. She insisted that it was a good gift and that any kid would want the dates. I had never seen dates before and I thought they looked strange but I knew better than to argue with Mom so I went to school with the wrapped box of dates. Fortunately, we didn't have to put our names on the gift. When the time came for us to draw a number and then pick a gift from the pile of wrapped Christmas gifts, I sat nervously waiting. I had already felt sorry for the kid who would pick the gift that I had brought. After everyone had picked out a gift, we were given the okay to unwrap our gifts. After a while, there was a commotion caused by one of the kids. It was a boy in the class.

"What is this!?" he exclaimed.

Some of the kids began to gather around him and then the teacher came over and saw what the boy was talking about. I sat there and remained still and quiet. I was too embarrassed to say anything and prayed that the teacher wouldn't ask who brought the gift. I was so angry with Mom! Why couldn't she just be a normal mother? Why did she have to be so stubborn and insist that everything be her way? And why was she so selfish and only care about herself and not care about me or what was going on with me? Fortunately, there were some extra gifts so the teacher gave the boy another gift. When I got home from school and told Mom about what happened at school. She said that the boy just didn't understand that the dates were a good gift. There was no point in reasoning with her. It was just impossible to do that.

One of my fondest memories of being in the fifth grade was when I got to take home a rabbit. The teacher in one of the classes I was in got us class rabbit and each student was able to take the rabbit home for one night. When it came to my turn, I walked home carrying the rabbit in its cage. As I was walking home, some of the other kids from school followed me. I felt so proud that I got to take the rabbit home. It was so neat to see other kids be interested in me even if it was because I had the rabbit. I enjoyed feeding the rabbit carrots and letting him out to eat grass. I also cleaned his cage with clean newspaper whenever he pooped in the cage. Sadly, the next morning I had to bring the rabbit back to class. I wished I could have kept the rabbit but of course, that wasn't possible.

Another short-lived but joyous memory was when I won a whole jar of candy. The school was having a fun fair day and one of the games we played was guessing how many candies were in a clear glass container. We had to write down the amount we thought were in the container. I guessed the exact amount, which was 41, and got to take the whole jar of candy home. I was so surprised when the teacher said my name. I had never won anything before. Usually, my brother James was considered the lucky kid because he would win prizes quite frequently.

When the fair came around every year, Dad would take James and me to go on the rides and play some of the games. Mom wouldn't always go with us for some reason. We never asked why Mom wasn't with us. We were just excited to be able to go. One time when she did come with us, there was a cake walk game in one of the booths. Mom decided that James and I should play because she wanted a cake. So we walked along the path of numbered squares while the music was playing. When the music stopped, we had to stop in the square that we were on. When they announced the winning number, it turned out that James was standing on the square with the winning number. Everyone cheered for him as he got to take home a chocolate cake.

Along with the fair, Dad liked to take me and James to do other fun things together. He would often get us up early on a

Saturday morning and we'd visit a local donut shop for some donuts. It would be just the three of us because Mom didn't like to get up that early. We would also go to the movies with Dad. I will never forget the time when he took us to see "Jaws". That movie terrified me and I heard people talk about it for a long time. They would say how unrealistic some of the scenes were and how the shark wasn't real. I chimed in myself as I learned more about how the movie was made. I guess by learning how it was filmed, it helped ease some of the fears about what I had seen in the movie.

# 4 The Power of Writing Things Down

I was about nine when I began Sunday school. I don't remember much from Sunday school except one Sunday, our teacher asked us to write down what we wanted to be when we got older. I had recently seen a police officer directing traffic in an intersection because the signal light was out and thought it looked like it would be fun, so I wrote down that I wanted to be a teacher or a police officer. I had no idea why I wrote down teacher since I cannot recall an experience, conversation, or image of why I would be inspired to become a teacher. Perhaps it was just my natural inclination.

One by one, the teacher asked each student what they wanted to be. When the teacher got to me, I told her that I wanted to be a teacher or police officer. The teacher asked, "Police Officer? Why would you want to be a Police Officer?"

"Because I saw a Police man in the street, telling this car to go there, and that car to go there," I explained as I motioned with my arms and hands extended out, "and I thought it looked like fun."

"You think that's fun?" the teacher asked sarcastically and condescendingly.

"Yes," I replied sheepishly and at the same time, slowly sunk lower into my seat.

Little did I know that nearly 20 years later, I would end up working as a Vocational Instructor at a Correctional Facility. Somehow, the combination of teaching in a law enforcement capacity working for the California Department of Corrections manifested to fulfill the answer I had written down years ago when I was a little girl in Sunday school. Although I don't recall having a strong desire to be a teacher or a police officer when I was instructed to write something down, I realized later that in order for any request made to God or the Universe to be fulfilled, you have to first know what you want. It's like not knowing what you want for Christmas so you most likely will get things you didn't want. Other than what I had written down on that little piece of paper, I grew up not really knowing what I wanted to be or do, because other than that Sunday school teacher, nobody ever asked me. I just sort of fell into this job or that job and eventually, fell into that Vocational Instructor position at the prison.

I also came to realize that after you write down your intentions, you have to let it go and release it. After that Sunday, I had no further thought of those words I'd written down. However, God or the Universe doesn't forget. That was the answer I had written, whether it was what I really wanted or not, and that's what was eventually delivered because I didn't clearly define what else I really wanted to be.

Often times, I am asked how I became a teacher in a prison and I would usually qualify my answer with, "Well, it's not like I grew up dreaming to be a teacher working in a prison." I didn't aspire to be a teacher in a prison. Yet, everything fell into place for me to fill that role. Out of six candidates who were interviewed, I was the one chosen. It started out with some friends who encouraged me to quit my job working for the Air Pollution Control District and go work for the Department of Corrections since, at the time, it was the largest growing State Department in California. They told me that because I was smart and had high work ethics, I would be able to move up the ladder quickly. My friends had a lot of confidence and belief in me and as it turned out, they were right. Things happened exactly as they said they would.

After I completed the lesson in Sunday School, my parents had me go through lessons for First Communion. I don't recall much from going through First Communion except that it was important to go to confession. We learned what to say and how to say it to the priest in the booth who was next to the one you were in. I thought it was strange to have to kneel down in a booth and practically whisper your sins to the faint outline of a man behind the screen. After finishing this "training" everyone in the church was to celebrate and honor those who completed the course. One evening, I was given a long white dress to wear, which was sown by our family seamstress, and a bouquet of flowers to hold. When we got to church, a lady and a fellow church member came up to me and placed a wreath of flowers on my head. After the ceremony, people, mostly adults, came up to me with beaming smiles, shook my hand and congratulated me. They seemed so happy for me. Yet, I had no idea what the ceremony was for, why I had to wear the white dress, and why I had flowers in my hair. My parents never told me why we were going to church that night and why I had to get dressed up. I just did as I was told.

Those were the simple and easier days for my parents. Life was good. They had one boy and one girl. Then they decided to have another child and that's when Dennis was born.

Before Dennis was born, my parents asked me and James if we wanted another baby brother or sister. I said I wanted a baby sister since I already had a younger brother. James said he wanted a baby brother. Prior to his arrival, my next door neighbor Gina and I would go see the baby that lived in the corner house of our street, who was about eight months old. He was already plump and filled out and Gina and I decided that he was the cutest baby in the world.

Then one day, when I came home from school, I was told that my new baby brother was sleeping in the crib in my parent's bedroom. I slowly and quietly opened the door and took a peek. There he was asleep. He had a very round head, his skin was reddish and he looked a little shriveled. I had never seen a new born before and thought he looked sort of ugly. However, over time, he began to fill out and soon *he* became the cutest baby in the world. He weighed 8 lbs. and 9 oz. at birth, which was large for a woman who was only 4'9". Mom had to have a cesarean to give birth to him. His birth and addition to the family caused my maternal instincts to kick in and I would often help with changing his diapers and watch after him, even though we already had a live in babysitter.

Dennis remained plump until he was almost four. We'd say that he was born with a beer belly. His head was shaped almost perfectly round and we would call him orange head. I guess that's what happens when a baby is born via cesarean since their heads didn't have to go through the birth canal. He was bald for a very long time and his hair crown was set right in the middle of the back of his head. Mom would say that if a child had two crowns, then they were like the Devil.

Dennis looked a lot like James when he was a baby. When you look at their baby pictures together, you would have thought they were twins. Yet they were actually six and a half years apart. However, Dennis came to have lighter colored hair with soft curls at the end, whereas James's hair remained darker with a slight wave. Until Dennis got his first haircut at age four, people would frequently mistake him for a little girl because of his soft curls. Once he got his first haircut though, the curls never came back.

When Dennis turned one year old our family had a big birthday party for him. When it came to him blowing out the candle for his cake, all the little kids kneeled at the coffee table where the round birthday cake was placed. Dennis was placed behind the cake and my brother James and I were on either side of Dennis, holding him up. Then all the other kids were kneeled next to James and me or standing behind us. Dennis became so excited about the cake and began waving his arms up and down. Then suddenly, he smacked the cake with his left hand, palm down and with a splat. Everybody thought it was funny and started laughing. My brother James and I then held his hands back so he wouldn't be able to do that again. We also helped him blow out his candle.

As Dennis was learning to walk, he was placed in a walker with a cloth seat and two holes for his legs to go through. The cloth seat was attached to a circular plastic ring that was attached to wheels that would roll on the ground. Dennis got to roam around outside in this walker. We lived in a duplex where two houses were joined at the garages. The garages were actually just covered carports, and both homes shared a wide driveway that sloped down to the street. One day, I was sitting outside crocheting and Dennis was out in his walker. Suddenly, I heard him crying. I immediately looked over to where he was and noticed that he had tipped himself upside down in his walker. He'd rolled himself over to the neighbor's yard and had gotten the walker stuck by a bush where the ground was lower and trimmed in a circular shape around the bush, almost as if the bush had a moat around it. His legs were kicking in the air and his perfectly round head was dangling upside down. His toothless mouth was wide open as he was crying. I was immediately concerned for him, of course, and ran over to help him but I also couldn't help but laugh hysterically because it was one of the funniest things I had seen.

Another time I was watching Dennis, I decided to take him with me into my parents' car. I was curious as to how the car worked. They had a Red Ford Cruisin' MI and it was parked facing the house. Our house out of the duplex was the one on the right. I had Dennis with me in the front seat that was one solid seat and didn't have a divider between the passenger and driver's seat. After pushing and pressing a few buttons, somehow, I had released the parking brakes. Suddenly, the car began to slowly roll backwards down the driveway at an angle and finally stopped when it hit some low hedges in the neighbor's front yard. The hedges were about two feet high and were lined along the sidewalk. Thankfully, the hedges were there to stop the car.

As it was rolling down the driveway, I began to panic. I didn't know how to stop the car from rolling. Once the car stopped I jumped out leaving Dennis inside. I don't remember why I left him in the car instead of taking him out with me but I knew I had to come up with an explanation. And I couldn't admit that I was the one that had caused the car to roll backwards or I would get severely punished. So as I was running up the driveway, which was about 50 feet towards the house, I had an idea. I thought I would say that Dennis had done something and that's how the car had started to move and roll backwards. That's it! So that was my explanation. Mom came out of the house, got in the car and drove it back to our side of the driveway. She didn't reprimand Dennis because he was only a baby. Whew! It worked. Thankfully, nobody got hurt since nobody was punished. And thankfully, she didn't even ask why we were in the car.

Dennis was left handed and this was a problem, at least to Mom. According to Mom, she believed that left-handed people were evil and she would often discipline him if she saw him using his left hand. She would sit by him as he wrote and would slap his left hand if he used it. Mom and Dad would argue about that. I felt really bad for him because Mom believed that way. I wanted her to leave him alone but wouldn't say anything for fear she would turn on me.

# 5 Like Mother Like Son

Even though the war was still going on in Vietnam, I had no clue of it. Then, when the Vietnam War ended, I heard adults begin talking about how Vietnam had opened their doors to allow Americans to enter the country again. That's when Dad went back to Vietnam to locate my grandmother and older brother Luc to bring them to the Philippines to come live with us. That's what many Vietnamese families do. They help bring their family members to be with them, so they can experience a better life. Dad was gone for a few weeks then finally came home empty-handed. He wasn't able to locate either my grandmother or Luc.

So Mom went back to locate them. News of what was going on in our family traveled, even in the neighborhood. One day, when I was outside drawing pictures with chalk on our driveway, a neighborhood boy came up to me and began to ask me questions. He was the older brother of one of the friends me and James played with so he wasn't someone I saw very often. As he sat next to me on the asphalt driveway, he asked me about my older brother, whom I remembered from Vietnam.

"So your mom went back to get your brother?" he asked.

"Yes."

"How old is your older brother?"

"He's eleven. He's really big. I remember him in Vietnam. He's going to come live with us," I said proudly. I had always wanted a bigger and older brother so that I could follow him around and learn from him.

"So did your family live in North Vietnam or South Vietnam?" he asked.

"North Vietnam," I replied, not knowing anything about the rivalry and conflict that occurred between the two sides. Why I thought we had lived in North Vietnam, I had no idea. It wasn't something my parents ever talked to us about. The neighbor kid asked me again.

"Are you sure you guys lived in North Vietnam?"

"Yes, it was North Vietnam."

"Okay. Well, it was nice talking to you."

I didn't know what I was talking about and later when I found out that we had actually lived in South Vietnam, I felt embarrassed. I wanted to tell that older neighbor kid that I was wrong but I never saw him again.

Unfortunately, Mom wasn't able to locate Grandmother either but she did find Luc and brought him back to live with the rest of the family. One day after school was over, I came home to find that Mom and Luc were back from Vietnam. My initial reaction when I saw Luc was one of surprise and disappointment. He didn't look the way I had expected him to. It had been five years since I last saw him and I thought he would be much taller. Instead, he was only about one inch taller than me and he didn't speak much English. He also had one crossed eye. Even though he was born with the one crossed eye, I never noticed it when I was younger and lived with him. I was four when I left Vietnam but now at age nine, I noticed his crossed eye. I was crushed and felt ashamed of him. He wasn't the older brother I had envisioned.

Mom and Dad told me to shake his hand so we shook hands quickly. Soon, he picked up from the look on my face that I was confused and disappointed. Of course it didn't help that I said to him, "Wow, you're not that tall." I'm not sure why I said that to him. I guess I was just so shocked that I expressed my thoughts out loud. He replied back mockingly, in his limited English to the effect that I wasn't tall either. I thought, *Well I'm not supposed to be tall. You're the older brother. You're supposed to be a lot taller than me.*

One day, I overheard my parents talk about what grade they would put Luc in. They talked about putting him in first grade because he didn't speak that much English. Then Dad said, "No. We can't do that. Let's put him in the same grade as Eden." I was horrified. *No!* I thought. I didn't want to see him in my classes or have anyone in school know he's my brother! I didn't say anything to my parents about how I felt because for some reason, I knew I was wrong for feeling embarrassed and ashamed of him. But I couldn't help it. I wanted someone older to learn from. Someone I could follow around and hang out with instead of my younger brother wanting to follow *me* and my friends around.

After a while Luc's English got better. Then my parents took him to the hospital to have surgery on his crossed eye. They didn't tell me or my brother James that's what they were going to do but one day, after coming home from school I noticed that Luc's eye had a glossy substance around it. It was the ointment that the doctors put on his eye after surgery. He had to continue putting on the ointment for a few days until it healed. I was glad that he got the surgery and that his English was getting better. However, his temper and attitude kept getting worse.

It didn't take long before our family felt the impact of having Luc in our lives. He was bitter and despised authority. When my parents were gone, he would get into fights with our maids and our babysitter because he refused to take any direction from them. He would respond by hitting, kicking, and talking back at them. While he was in Vietnam, he learned Karate and felt that he was tougher than anyone. In Vietnam, he had limited supervision and guidance by my grandmother and other relatives. One time, he ended up seriously hurting our maid by kicking her in the groin area so she threatened to quit working for our family. He would also pick on James and me, often teasing us, belittling us, and mocking us. One morning as I was getting dressed in the bathroom, Luc opened the door and began mocking me. It seemed that he really knew how to push our buttons. I became so angry with him that I chased him out of the house and down the street. But he was too fast. I fell on the street and scraped my chest and knees. Then I realized that I had run out of the house without a shirt on. As I picked myself up from the asphalt. I yelled angrily, "I'm going to get you!" When I got back home, my friend Melissa, who had stayed the night at our house, was laughing and said, "I can't believe you ran out of the house without your shirt on!" "Well, he made me mad," I mumbled.

Another time, Mom had taken all of us kids with her to stop by one of her friend's house. It was late and already dark so she had my brothers and me wait in the car. We were all sitting in the back seat and soon Luc started to pick on James. Soon, they began hitting each other back and forth and I told James, "Get him!" Then they both got out of the car while still wrestling and hitting each other. Suddenly, the car door opened on the side where I had been sitting and I started feeling somebody punching me. It was Luc. He kept punching, hitting, and kicking me with his feet in the head, body, or anywhere he could. I felt so helpless because I couldn't fight back. I tried blocking some of the blows but the blows kept coming. Finally, when he had let all his anger out, he stopped. I realized immediately that he didn't like it when I encouraged James to win against him.

Telling Mom about it did little to keep him from behaving violently towards James and me and she offered no comfort to us for having to be the subject of his wrath. She felt sorry for him, which at the time, I couldn't understand why. I asked Mom one day, "Why do you let Luc drink sodas all the time when James and I can only have them only sometimes?" She replied, "Because I feel sorry for him."

Luc's violence and anger didn't just end in our household. It seemed that no matter where we went, he would somehow end up getting in a fight with another kid at school or anywhere else.

One time, Dad had dropped off Luc, James, and me at Pool No. 2 on base. There were three pools on base and Pool No. 2 had a larger pool where it was deeper and where adults and older kids would swim. Then there was a smaller pool where it was shallower and where most of the younger kids would swim. That's where my brothers and I would swim. Before long, Luc began fighting with another kid in the pool. I was a few feet away from them and so I yelled at Luc to stop. Suddenly Luc turned on me and pushed my head under the water. I tried raising my head, splashing and kicking, and reaching for his hand, but he was much stronger than me and kept holding me under. All the while, I'm thinking, *He is trying to drown me!* I reached a point where I felt I couldn't hold my breath any longer. Finally, he let me go. I pulled up out the water gasping for air. I began to cry, feeling once again angry, humiliated and powerless. A few seconds longer, I would have drowned. Telling my parents brought little consequence to him and no condolences to me. It seemed he could get away with anything.

Even in junior high school, after we had moved to the U.S., Luc would get into fights with other kids. It seemed he was constantly trying to prove how good he was in Karate or just wanted to challenge the other boys to prove how tough he was. Soon, he became known throughout the school for always getting into fights. This continued to foster the shame and resentment I felt towards him. During a lunch break, one of the girls in the school approached me and asked, "Is Luc your brother?"

I reluctantly said, "Yes. Why?"

She replied, "I feel sorry for him."

I looked at her and noticed how pretty she was. I couldn't understand why a pretty girl like her would feel sorry for my brother.

I replied, "I don't. He's the one getting himself into all those fights."

"I know but I still feel sorry for him," she calmly replied.

It wasn't until years later that I was able to imagine what Luc may have gone through when he had to stay behind in Vietnam while James and I left with our parents to the Philippines. I heard that he wasn't well supervised by my grandmother or relatives and had joined some street gangs but how true that is, I don't know. I didn't know there were gangs in Vietnam. At the very least, I am certain that he had to have felt abandoned by his family. How could a six year old understand why he couldn't be with his mother, father, and siblings? Being left behind in Vietnam evidently made him jealous of James and me. And Dennis wasn't left out either. Luc was not affectionate towards Dennis like everyone else was and soon it became evident that he was jealous of Dennis too.

One evening, when we were living in California and when Dennis was only two, I saw Luc do something so disturbing that it clearly showed his hatred for himself. After all, why would anyone try to hurt someone else, especially an innocent baby, unless they were miserable and didn't feel good about them self? I didn't put this connection together until the writing of this book because many of these memories had been buried and almost forgotten. And this incident was one of the many things that I had to forgive Luc for. I never told Dennis what Luc had done to him when he was a baby. I realized it wasn't something he needed to know. Besides, I had to focus on my own survival so I subconsciously buried this memory for good, so I thought.

That evening, Dad had put Dennis in the bath tub and started the water for Dennis to take a bath. The door was opened since Dennis still needed to be supervised. Dad had left the bathroom for some reason. As I walked by the bathroom and looked inside, I was horrified by what I saw Luc doing. He had a gallon of bleach and was pouring it over Dennis's head. As I watched Luc, I questioned if I was seeing things correctly. Then Luc took a can of Clorox cleansing powder and sprinkled it over Dennis's head on top of the bleach he had already poured. Suddenly, I came to my senses. I immediately felt so much anger and rage towards Luc that I almost couldn't talk. Dennis began to cry and started rubbing his eyes because the bleach had gotten into them.

"What are you doing!?" I demanded, my voice screeching and cracking. "Dad!"

Dad came over and asked what happened.

"Luc poured bleach over Dennis's head and then he put Clorox on top!" I exclaimed.

I could barely get the words out and was almost hyperventilating because I was so shocked by what I had seen. I couldn't move to stop Luc either. It was as if I was paralyzed. Either I was afraid to approach Luc for fear he would beat me up or I was so stunned by the scene. By that time I was crying because I just couldn't understand why Luc would do such a thing.

What sick person would do such a thing to anyone, let alone a baby that was your own brother?

Dad looked down to see the gallon of bleach and the can of Clorox cleanser on the side of the bathtub. "Why did you do that?!" Dad yelled at Luc. "What did you do that for?!" Dad kept asking as he began to hit Luc. As Dad kept beating Luc, Luc kept saying, "I don't know!" while trying to shield himself from the blows. As Luc moved out of the bathroom while Dad continued to beat him, I rushed over to Dennis and began to wash the bleach and Clorox cleanser off his head, trying not to get it into his eyes. I was sobbing because I was afraid that the bleach could have damaged Dennis's eyes and blinded him. But he was okay and thankfully didn't go blind. I don't know if Luc understood what he had done and why he was punished for it. I felt that he deserved the punishment and that hopefully, he learned his lesson to never do anything like that again.

Behaviors such as these, including his bullying, selfishness, and rudeness made me resent Luc even more. It got to the point where I couldn't stand to be in the same room as him. We didn't talk to each other and avoided each other like the plague. When it was his turn to help me with the dishes after dinner, I couldn't bear standing next to him. It didn't dawn on me until I became an adult that I had the same feelings about Luc that I did for Mom. When I learned the meaning of the word "loathe" in school and had to use it in a sentence, I said that I loathed my brother, referring to Luc. The teacher replied, "Oh dear."

At the time, I couldn't understand his anger and didn't link the similarities in his temperament to Mom's until years later. Even when I learned about what he may have gone through by being left in Vietnam, I felt that it still didn't justify his actions and made it okay for him to behave violently towards others. It seemed he just had no tolerance for anyone in authority and he was always pushing people's buttons, challenging them, teasing and belittling them. He also thought he knew everything and that he was always right. He knew the best colleges to go to, the best sports teams, and the best career to go into. There wasn't anything he didn't know. It was a wonder that he had any friends, but he did manage to have a few.

Needless to say, when Luc left to join the military after we graduated high school, our relationship was so strained that we were not on talking terms. After a few years, I learned he had gotten out of the Air Force and was living in Napa, California. I decided to let by-gones be by-gones and reached out to him, after getting his phone number from Dad, in an attempt to reconcile. I had learned about forgiveness and I told him that it didn't matter about the past that we should just try to get along moving forward. I told him I would come visit him. I was still living in Merced at the time and would've driven the two plus hours to see him. However, he made every excuse as to why I couldn't come visit him. Either he was too busy or he wouldn't be at home that weekend. I didn't understand. Later, I realized that he may have been ashamed of the place he was living in.

Then, in our second phone conversation, where I was still trying to make amends, he verbally attacked and made fun of me, criticizing me for wanting to reconcile. "You want to live in a Utopia! You're an idiot!" he said mockingly and condescendingly. I couldn't believe it. His anger and words brought me to tears. I guess to him, wanting to forgive others and get along with them in peace was stretching my imagination and living in a dream world, which evidently was different from his perspective of the world. Needless to say, I didn't speak to him or see him again until Mom died four years later. After that, I never saw or spoke to him again. I decided that it wasn't worth it. I'd done all I could.

# 6 From Luxury to Slavery

When my parents told us we were moving to the United States and in particular to California, James and I were very excited. We were in the car on our way to Church. I began imagining places like San Francisco, Los Angeles or Sacramento, places I had heard of or learned in school. I also thought of snow and recalled the slides from school of the beautiful colors of the leaves during the fall. We had learned about the different seasons and what the U. S. looked like during those seasons.

"What town are we moving to?" I asked.

"Merced," Dad answered.

"Merced? Where's that?"

"It's in California."

"Does it snow there?"

"No, it doesn't snow there?"

"How can it not snow there? We learned in school about the four seasons in the United States and in the winter time it snows," I insisted.

"Well, it doesn't snow there," Dad replied.

Later, I looked at a map of California and found where Merced was. Okay, so it wasn't one of those cities I'd heard of but it was still in the U. S. and that was exciting enough.

Then Mom said, "You know, they don't have maids in the United States. Who's going to clean the house?"

*"I* will!" I excitedly volunteered.

I had always wanted to help around the house since we always had a maid that cleaned the house. Labor in the Philippines was very cheap and Mom lived like a queen. At times we would also have a live in babysitter when Dennis was born. Then Mom had a hair stylist, a manicurist, and a seamstress that would come to the house to provide services for her. We also had yard boys, which is equivalent to a gardener here in the U.S.

Even though we had maids, I still couldn't understand how our house was always clean because I never actually saw the maids cleaning the house. I figured they must have done a lot of the cleaning before my brothers and I woke up. Sometimes the maids would go to their own homes over the weekend but most of the time the maids were there to tuck us into bed and were there when we woke up. Sometimes they had their own bedroom or they would sleep on a separate bed in my room.

Since the maids always did the cooking and the dishes, I wanted to know what it would be like to wash dishes and do chores around the house. I wasn't sure if I thought it was fun or just wanted to experience doing something an adult did, so I would sometimes beg my parents to let me wash the dishes, which they allowed me to do at times.

Nevertheless, when Mom asked who was going to clean the house, little did I know that whether I volunteered or not, my parents had already decided I was going to be the one to do all the choirs around the house, including the cooking, because I was a girl.

Finally, the day came for us to move. I asked Dad if we were bringing our toys with us. Dad replied in a stern tone, "No, we don't have room." I felt sad that we couldn't bring our toys with us. The impact of not having our toys was felt even heavier when we arrived in the U.S. and got settled into our new house. There was nothing to remind me of my childhood. All my Barbie dolls, stuffed animals and other toys were gone. It was as if overnight, I went from being a tomboy to a girl and from a child to an adult.

I was ten when we moved to the U.S. Luc was twelve, James was eight, and Dennis was almost two. In the beginning, we would ask Dennis where Lydia, our last maid in the Philippines was. Dennis would raise both his hands and wave them back and forth and say, "Lydia all gone." After a while, we stopped asking him and he eventually forgot who she was.

When we first arrived in California, we lived in an apartment in a small town called Atwater near Castle AFB where Dad was stationed. Although there was only one month left in the school year, Dad enrolled us to go to school. We begged him to just give us the summer off instead of going to school but he wouldn't allow it. So we went to school for one month. Luc and I were enrolled in the 5th grade and James was enrolled in 3rd.

The schools we attended on Castle AFB were much more advanced than the public schools in the U.S., as I soon found out. By the 5th grade, I already knew how to add and subtract fractions with ease. One day in my math class at the public school I attended in Atwater, the teacher wrote a mixed fraction problem on the black board and asked the students in class how to solve it. After several seconds, I was the only hand that was raised. The teacher called on me and asked me to explain how to solve the problem. I then proceeded to solve the problem. The teacher said, "You see, Eden had to come all the way from the Philippines just to show you guys how to do fractions." I slowly sunk in my chair. I didn't mean to be a show off and I certainly didn't want anyone else to feel bad for not knowing how to solve the problem.

During our lunch break, some of us would play baseball. One day, a group of us decided to play. While I was helping to get everyone situated and organized into teams, one kid started to pitch the ball to another kid who was already stationed at home base. I was standing right behind the girl that was all ready to swing the ball and as soon as I saw the pitch, I put my hands out in front of me and yelled out, "Wait!" but it was too late. The girl in front of me swung the bat back, not realizing I was right behind her, and hit my left hand, spraining my pinky, ring, and middle fingers. Nobody was in position and the teams hadn't been picked yet so I don't know why they decided to start playing.

After the girl, who swung the bat, realized that she had hit my hand, she apologized profusely. I accepted her apologies and was thankful that I didn't get hit somewhere else, like in my head. My three fingers were swollen for several days. Thank goodness it was my left hand and not my right. I wasn't sure if they were broken or not but when I showed them to Dad and explained to him during dinner that evening what happened at school, he was unmoved and just dismissed the incident. "Ah, they're probably just sprained. You'll be fine," he said callously.

I thought, *How would he know? Is he a doctor? Why did I even bother telling him?* I had a feeling he would just dismiss it. I soon learned that he didn't want to be bothered with anything that might cause him to spend money, like a visit to the doctor's office. Instead of showing my disappointment to his reaction, I just stuffed my feelings and acted as if I never said anything at all. I had to be tough; I couldn't show him how discouraged I felt that I wasn't important enough for him to even take a look at my fingers.

When we lived in the apartment, there were a couple of neighbor kids that we would play with. One day, we saw our neighborhood friends and asked if they wanted to play. One of the boys said, "We can't play right now because we're going to 7-Eleven."

"What? What do you mean seven eleven?" We had no concept of what 7-Eleven was since living on Castle Air Base, we had never heard of 7-Eleven as the name of a convenience store. To us, 7-Eleven were just two numbers.

"You know, 7-Eleven."

"What's seven eleven?"

"It's a store."

"How can seven eleven be a store? Those are just numbers."

"It's the name of the store."

"Oh."

We also didn't have McDonalds, Pizza Hut, or any of the fast food restaurants on base. However, we quickly learned and became fond of all the new foods we were eating, especially McDonalds.

When we lived in the Philippines, the closest we came to pizza was Chef Boyardee out of a box that Dad would make. We loved his pizza and when we first ate at Pizza Hut, I actually didn't like the pizza. I preferred Dad's "homemade" pizza and told him so. However, there would be no more "homemade" pizza. We lived in America now and there was no need to make pizza when we can just buy it. Besides, Dad didn't have extra time like he used to. Besides work, he was taking classes at night, and then had other responsibilities around the house like yard work, since we no longer had a yard boy. Over time though, my taste buds acquired the taste for pizza from the fast food restaurants and soon, I had forgotten all about Dad's "homemade" pizza.

The other great thing about living in the apartment complex was the swimming pool. Although there were signs around the pool area and outside the pool gate that said adult supervision was required, Dad still gave us the key to the gate so we could go swimming. Mom was not home much and Dad worked. He also had other things to attend to that left Luc in charge of us in the pool area. Dennis, who was only two, was most likely with Mom, wherever she may be. Oftentimes, we never knew where she was. Our parents didn't always tell us where they would be and of course, there were no cell phones to call them in case of an emergency.

So swimming was one of the best ways our parents found to keep us occupied. Luc, James, and I loved swimming and it didn't matter that it would be later in the evening and the sun was no longer around. There was still daylight and even though the water temperature in the pool was freezing cold, we would swim until our teeth chattered and our skin turned blue. On many occasions, we were the only kids or tenants in the pool. One day though, we got caught. A tenant saw that we didn't have any adult supervision and told us that we needed to have our parents with us. Later, we told Dad about the encounter with the tenant that scolded us for being in the pool area without adult supervision. Dad just shrugged it off and said, "It doesn't matter. You guys have been swimming there by yourselves all this time anyway." So we had to sneak into the pool area from that point on.

After school was over, we lived in the apartment for another month or so. Then we moved from the apartment to a house in Merced. It was a in a newer subdivision and I still recall the large bill board sign, advertising the new homes for $26,000 in that subdivision. When we moved into our new home, I was disappointed. It was smaller than the last home we lived in on Clark Air Base. For some reason and at only ten, I thought my parents could have done better. I thought we could have had a bigger home and lived in a nicer area, like the one in the Philippines. I didn't understand why my parents choose this house instead of a bigger house and in a better neighborhood. I didn't realize that things were more expensive living in the U.S. Our house in the Philippines had lighter colored tiled floors. This house had dark olive green carpet with linoleum flooring in the kitchen and bathrooms. Also, the back yards had fencing around them. Our homes in the Philippines didn't have fencing in the back yard, which allowed us to roam all over the neighborhood.

Our home in Merced was also only three bedrooms like the one on base but because I was a girl and getting older, my parents had me in my own bedroom while my three brothers had to share a room. James and Dennis slept on bunk beds while Luc had a twin bed. My parents also got me a canopy bed with a butterfly themed canopy, bed spread, and bed ruffle. I loved my canopy bed but felt sad that they chose to buy me "things" instead of showing me affection and spending time with me. Not that I wanted Mom to be home because if she were, she would reprimand and lecture me for no reason. But somehow, I felt that I was being bought. I wanted my parents to be home so they could spend time with me and my brothers and for them to be loving, even though I didn't know exactly what that looked like. I became resentful that I had a nice bedroom set but had to be the mother of the house or even the slave.

By that time, my parents had taught me how to cook, dust, vacuum, clean the bathroom, and do the laundry. I didn't mind at first since cooking and cleaning was all new to me and in my mind, kind of fun. I never got to do those things in the Philippines. Even when my brothers were watching television and I was the only one doing the choirs, it didn't bother me. However, after we moved from the apartment into our new home in Merced, and when school began again, I found that I had a hard time keeping up with all the chores. That's when I began to realize that I was the only one required to do the cooking and cleaning. Then there was homework from school and also helping my younger brother James with his homework.

While I was doing chores or cooking, my brothers would be outside playing or watching TV. Luc was a huge sports fan and he would often sit right in front of the TV, turning the dial from channel to channel so he could watch several games at a time. Nobody would ask to watch something if he was in front of the TV because he would get mad and we knew that if he got upset, he would beat us up.

Mom was gone a lot to who knows where. Sometimes she wouldn't even come home to sleep. Dad worked and went to school in the evenings so he wasn't home much either. As soon as I got home from school, I had to start dinner. What to cook for dinner was usually started with a phone call from Mom, giving me instructions on what to cook. I would often make stir fry and then there was always rice cooked in a rice cooker to go with it.

If dinner wasn't ready by 5 PM when Dad got home, he would demand, "Where's dinner!" All the while, my brothers would be outside playing football or some other game with the other neighbor boys. Then, when dinner was ready, I would call them in to eat. Soon, I began to resent having to do all the chores and even after cooking dinner every night, I had to wash the dishes. I thought, *How dare Dad demands dinner from me as if I was his wife! Where's Mom, your real wife? She's the one that should be doing this and not your 11-year-old daughter!* But there was no sense in saying those things since I would get a beating for sure.

However, I did start to complain and plead my case that it wasn't fair for me to do all the chores while my brothers could be outside playing. Finally, my parents decided that my brothers should help with the cleanup after dinner. James and Luc would have to alternate every other day and help me wash the dishes. I still had to wash or rinse the dishes, depending on whether James or Luc washed or rinsed the dishes. It wasn't exactly what I was looking for but I realized that this was going to be the best I could get as far as help goes.

When I needed help with my homework and asked Dad for assistance, he would reply, "Oh, it's been a long time since I've done Algebra. I can't remember any of that," which disappointed me. I had been one of the few students that was placed in an Algebra class in Junior High and if I could pass the assessment test at the end, I would be able to skip Algebra in High School and move on to Geometry. But without any help from home, there was no way I was able to pass the assessment test.

The Algebra teacher, Mr. Lusk, was a mild mannered, older teacher and the kids took advantage of that. They wouldn't listen to him, often interrupting and making fun of him. Mr. Lusk would get flustered and turn beet red but he never got angry with the kids. He tried so hard to maintain control but the kids took all the control. These kids, including myself, were all considered advanced when it came to our math competency and that's why we were placed in that special class. It was sort of like a pilot program and they were doing this at other junior high schools, but it didn't work out. It was too difficult for me to understand Mr. Lusk because he kept getting distracted by the kids that were taunting and teasing him.

Finally, when we were tested on our Algebra competency, only three students, who were all girls, out of thirty passed. I was disappointed that I didn't pass the exam and I wanted to know how the three students who did pass it were able to. So I asked them how they were able to pass. They all told me that they received assistance from their parents. One of the girl's fathers was a mathematician at the high school in town and he was able to help her with her homework. I thought, *I knew it! If only I had some help from Dad (there was no way I would even consider asking Mom for help), I could have passed the assessment test just like those three students did.*

Sadly, the disruptive behavior of the majority of the students in the class came back to bite them. It was a waste of the teacher's time and of the students' since we had to take the Algebra class again in high school. It was also too bad that Mr. Lusk couldn't admit to the Principal that he was losing control over the class. Perhaps if they had known sooner, they could have brought in another teacher to teach the Algebra class. We heard that after that class, Mr. Lusk retired. I couldn't blame him.

# 7 Confession, Lies, and Hypocrisy

Dad worked during the day and took evening classes during the week so he could obtain his Engineering degree, which meant that he wasn't home much. However, Mom was gone a lot too. There are times when she wouldn't even come home at night and I didn't know where she would be. She would call home after school and give me directions as to what to cook for dinner but that was about it. Then one weekend, she took us kids to the base bowling alley. She told us that we were going to meet one of her friends. I was eleven and because I was very small for my age, she told me that if her friend asked me how old I was, I was to say that I was nine.

When I first saw Todd, I noticed that he was younger, at least younger than Dad. It wasn't that Mom looked very old but she was Mom and was married with children. Why would this young man be interested in her? People would comment about how young Mom looked but why would this guy be attracted to a woman with four kids?

As we were driving to the Base, Todd eventually asked me how old I was. I told him I was nine and immediately felt weird about telling him that. Then he asked what grade I was in. Then Mom chimed in, "She in sixth grade." Todd looked at me again. "She very smart," Mom replied.

When we got to the Base, Todd, showed us how well he played pin ball. We were at the bowling alley and there was an area where there were several pin ball machines. As my brothers and I leaned on the pin ball machine and watched in awe, he asked us to not lean on the machine so that he could jiggle the pin balls to his advantage to get them into the slot. After bowling, Todd took us back home. Even though we never saw

Todd again, I still wondered about him and Mom. Mom acted different around Todd and I had a feeling it was more than just a friendship. She seemed more airy, and she laughed and smiled more. It seemed strange.

One night at around 11 PM, while I was lying in bed trying to go to sleep, I heard the phone ring. Dad answered the phone. Suddenly, I heard him yell, "She's not here! You stop calling for her you hear me?!" It must have been Todd. Mom wasn't home as usual, and was probably staying at a friend's house. Wow! That was sure bold of Todd to actually call late at night when he knew Mom was married.

Then, at times when Mom was home, I would hear her and Dad fighting and yelling at each other in their bedroom. As I lay in bed, I would pray that they don't get a divorce. "Please God; please don't let them get a divorce."

I later asked Mom if she was going to divorce Dad. She said, "No, I never divorce your dad. Because Catholics, we don't get divorced." I was relieved because I was afraid that if they were to get divorced, I would be stuck with Mom and then there really wouldn't be anyone to protect me. I was afraid that my younger brothers would be able to go with Dad and me and Luc, whom I didn't get along with either, would have to go with Mom. And *that* would make things worse. My life would be even more miserable than it already was if that were to happen. Thankfully it didn't. But how hypocritical of her to say she wouldn't divorce Dad when she's the one befriending another man. It wasn't that he was younger, it was because she was married. Also, if you're going to be saying you're Catholic and go to church and go to confession, then why didn't she do the things that Catholics were supposed to do and believe in?

Somewhere along the way, I learned that the wife was supposed to be in submission to her husband and that the husband was the head of the household. Where I learned that, I don't recall. Perhaps it was in Sunday school or from going to church, or perhaps Mom even told me that. But certainly, that's not what she practiced. Mom was very independent and I admired her for being adventurous enough and not being afraid to drive hundreds of miles to Lake Tahoe, Reno, and Las Vegas to gamble at the casinos in those cities.

Even though we lived in Merced, we would still go to the church on base every Sunday. There was a tradition during mass to turn around and shake the hand of the people around you. Often, we would see families hugging and kissing each other. Clearly there was a lot of love in those families and displays of affection were obviously very natural and normal for them. That definitely wasn't the case in our family. It seemed that Mom craved and longed for her children to show love and affection towards her but how was that possible when she didn't teach us that? Since she didn't show us love and affection, it was difficult for us to show love towards her. It was especially hard for me.

One Sunday, I was sitting next to Mom. Dad was not with us for some reason. The priest then told us to standup. By that time, I knew what was coming. What I didn't expect was for Mom to lean into my ear and whisper to me, "Give me a kiss." I immediately felt sick to my stomach. Affection between us was nonexistent and now she wants me to do what? I could see right through her and knew she wanted others to see how much her kids loved her. However, I waited to see if she asked my brothers to do the same but she didn't. Why me?! So I leaned over and gave her a kiss on the cheek, which made me feel disgusted. How dare she be so hypocritical, demanding I show her affection and love when she never showed it towards me?

Having gone through First Communion, Mom began taking Luc, James, and me to confession on Saturdays. She never took confession with us. If she did go, it was on her own. By then, things had changed in how we were supposed to confess. Instead of entering a small booth and speaking to the priest in the next booth, you actually sat in a room with the priest and confessed your sins that way. So one Saturday afternoon, Mom took us to confession. However, before we went into the room, she coached me on what to say and what to confess. She would pull me to the side and whisper in my ear to tell me that I was to tell the priest that I had lied to her, that I was being a disobedient daughter, and that I fought with my brothers. Even though I didn't feel that it was true, I had to confess something and she couldn't just let me say what I wanted. She always told me what to say. I wondered if she did the same thing to my brothers, although I don't recall ever seeing her do that to them.

"So you would lie to your mother and fight with your brothers?" the priest asked.

"Yes," I replied.

Thankfully, he didn't ask for specifics because I would have to make something up. The only brother I fought with was my older brother Luc even though he was the one that would provoke the fighting. I learned to stay out of his way but he had a way of getting angry easily like Mom and would lash out by beating me or my other brothers. So if your older brother beats up on you, would that be considered fighting with your brothers? When we were finished, Mom asked me what the priest said.

"He told me to say three Hail Marys and two Our Fathers," which I would do while kneeling down on the kneelers in the church.

Although Dad was raised Protestant in Germany, he attended church with us just to please Mom and to keep peace in the family. Mom kept hoping that eventually Dad would become a Catholic and insisted that he come with us, which he often did. However, Dad admitted that he was never going to be a Catholic. Yet he agreed with almost everything Mom wanted.

After going to church on base for a while, my parents decided to have my brothers become altar boys. The priest told my parents that if Luc and James were going to be altar boys, they had to get nicer shoes instead of wearing tennis shoes. My parents couldn't afford to buy dress shoes for my brothers but somehow, they were still allowed to be altar boys. I guess the priest figured that their shoes wouldn't show underneath the robes, but they did. It wasn't so much that my brothers wore tennis shoes under their robes that bothered me. What bothered me was how my brothers acted outside of church. More specifically Luc.

James and I were taught not to curse or call each other "stupid", but here Luc, who was supposed to be an altar boy would curse and act violently if he didn't get his way. Somehow that just didn't seem right to me and I felt that his behavior was hypocritical.

Another occurrence that seemed questionable to me when we went to church had to do with a certain priest. Even though we attended church every Sunday, there were a few different priests that would hold mass there. There was one in particular that I will never forget. It seemed that while he was giving his sermon, he would often look at a lady and her daughter that sat in the front row of the church. He would look at them and smile at them quite often. It was as if he was mesmerized and he couldn't help himself. I don't know if the mother didn't have a husband because I never saw a man sitting next to her, but they were there pretty regularly and they always sat in the front row of pews. It seemed that this priest had a fondness for either the mother or the daughter, who was in the age range of 16 to 20. However, my suspicion and feeling was that he really liked the daughter. I had learned that priests weren't supposed to get married and that wasn't what bothered me. I just couldn't understand why this priest made his fondness for this lady or her daughter so obvious. I wondered if anyone else noticed him looking at them all the time. But I never mentioned my suspicions to anyone. There were a lot of things that I just kept to myself.

# 8 "Envy is Ignorance" ~Ralph Waldo Emerson

During our second summer in California, our parents took us to see Mom's second cousin who lived in Oxnard. Even though they were cousins, we had to address her as Auntie Lily out of respect. Auntie Lily had three girls and one son. One of the daughters, Catherine was married to a Caucasian American man named Mike, who already had children from his first wife. Mike had one son that was already grown and living on his own, then he had two sons and a daughter still growing up and living with him and Catherine. They also had one girl together. Mike's children from his first wife all had blond hair and blue eyes. My brothers and I would play with Mike's children, who were mostly older. We had a lot of fun playing with them, like hide and go seek, which we would play outside and around the house. They also took us to the beaches in the Oxnard and Ventura area.

As we spent more time with our distant cousins that week, I developed a mild crush on one of them, Mark, who was probably around 16. There was something about his almost shoulder length blond hair and his sparkling blue eyes. I also liked how mature he seemed, taking us around to see the sights of the area. However, I quickly dismissed any feelings or thoughts of liking him because after all, he was a relative, even if it was only by marriage. Besides, I was much too young to develop any type of romantic relationship and I knew it.

Auntie Lily had another daughter who wasn't married but had a boyfriend. They weren't as approving of Emily's life style because she wasn't married. I would overhear Mom and Auntie Lily talk about Emily because she had several boyfriends over the years but wasn't married yet. The youngest daughter had the same name as Mom's and she and I got close for a while.

We stayed in Oxnard for several days, sleeping at Auntie Lily's two bedroom apartment that was on the second level. My parents slept in one of the rooms and Auntie Lily slept in the other room. My brothers and I, along with Cousin Lucy all slept on the living room floor or on the couch.

When we first arrived to Auntie Lily's apartment, Dennis had gotten really sick, having contracted the flu. He had a fever, was throwing up and also had diarrhea. Dennis was miserable and I felt so bad for him. My heart ached for him. He kept walking around the apartment crying, "I'm going to die Mamma. I'm going to die." I wondered how this almost three year old toddler would know what death was. Mom would chuckle at him when he said that, which annoyed me. Perhaps she thought it was cute coming from him but instead of holding him in her lap and consoling him, which I thought she should have done, she laughs at him. Thankfully, he got better.

One night, while everyone had fallen asleep, James and I stayed up watching Creature Feature, which was featuring a movie called "Children Shouldn't Play With Dead Things". As James and I laid on the make shift beds made for us on the living room floor and with all the lights off except for the flickering light given off by the TV, we tensely watched the movie about Zombies coming out of the graves to attack a small group of people who landed on a remote island. Even though we were so frightened by many of the horrifying scenes, we couldn't turn the TV off. Somehow, we watched the entire movie and when it was over, we both vowed to never watch a scary or horror movie again.

"That was so scary!" I whispered.

"I know," James said.

"I am never going to watch another scary movie again."

"Me either."

Then somehow, we managed to fall asleep. During the day, Mom, Aunt Lily and the adult kids like Lucy and Emily would sit in a circle on the carpeted living room floor playing Chinese cards and talk. I would sit on the floor with them and just watch them play even though I couldn't understand what they were talking about since they were talking in Vietnamese. Being around my adult cousins was all new to me. But this bothered Mom. For some reason, she didn't want me around so she told me in an annoyed tone, "Why don't you go outside and play." I couldn't understand why this would bother her since I wasn't talking or making any noise to distract them.

So I replied, "I just want to watch what you guys are doing."

Normally, I wouldn't "talk back" like that but figured she wasn't going to do anything in front of everyone. However, it didn't take long before I got bored. So I went outside to swim and see what the other kids were doing. Besides, it was uncomfortable staying where you weren't wanted.

There was a swimming pool at Auntie Lily's apartment complex and since it was summer, it was a great time to go swimming. One time I was out by the pool with my cousin Lucy and cousin Mark whom I had the crush on. Even though I had my bathing suit on, I was too embarrassed to go swimming. Lucy kept urging me to get into the pool but I couldn't. I didn't want to swim in front of Mark. So I sat by the edge of the pool with my feet in the water and just hung out as they talked, wishing that I was older. Soon, Mark decided to go up to Auntie Lily's apartment but not without first tossing in a quarter into the pool and telling me that I could have it if I could swim down to the bottom and retrieve it. After he was out of sight, I finally got into the swimming pool and swam down to the deeper end and retrieved the coin. I wasn't the best swimmer since I couldn't float very well, but I could hold my breath and stay under water for a while. After a little while, Mark came back down and while I was still in the pool, I showed him the quarter I had retrieved. "Good job!" he said. Then he left to go home.

Cousin Lucy would come visit us in Merced and she would sleep with me in my room. As we were going to sleep, Lucy and I would stay up very late and talk. Lucy would tell me how much Mom loved me. I couldn't believe it when she told me that. I told her how Mom treated me and said emphatically, "Well if she does love me, she has a funny way of showing it." Lucy would try to explain Mom's viewpoint but I couldn't accept it. Even though I didn't know what it was like to feel or to be shown love, I knew this wasn't the way to do it.

Lucy also confessed that she believed that Mom was jealous of her. This was because of how Dad would tease and joke around with Lucy. I saw how Dad did this but I never thought it was anything unusual and never felt he was being flirtatious with Lucy. Dad would joke around at times with other people, like company or friends that my parents would have over. What was wrong with that? How could Mom be jealous of her own niece? Was it because he was giving Lucy attention instead of her? Mom could get more attention from Dad had she been home more. Eventually, we came to the conclusion that Mom was also jealous of me.

Lucy came over another time and stayed with us awhile. This time though, she spent some time with Todd. I guess Mom had tried setting up Lucy with Todd, but he really wasn't interested in Lucy. He was more interested in Mom even though she had four kids. Eventually Lucy did get married to a Caucasian man who had the same last name as Dad's. In fact the spelling was exactly the same. I was happy that Lucy found someone because I felt bad that Todd didn't like her the way he liked Mom.

It had been a couple of years now since I had worn a dress. I didn't like wearing them because of that little boy in first grade that kept lifting my dress up in school. But Dad had a friend from the Air Force that he wanted to visit. His friend Doug lived in Santa Barbara, which was a beautiful town along the coast of California, with his beautiful airline stewardess wife, although today they are called flight attendants. Mom wanted to make a good impression on them so Mom bought me a dress to wear. Although I was only 11, I felt so much older because of all the responsibilities that were heaped upon me and I no longer saw myself as a little girl. Yet the style of dress Mom bought was certainly for a little girl. It had short capped sleeve, a reddish orange background with a print, and it hung several inches above my knees. It was as if the dress was too small for me. I had been wearing pants for so long that I wasn't used to having my legs exposed like that except if I was wearing shorts. But I didn't have a choice. Even though I protested and said I didn't want to wear the dress, Mom insisted that I wear it. So the whole day of wearing that dress, I felt extremely uncomfortable.

After an almost five hour drive, we arrived at Doug's and Jennifer's beautiful house in Santa Barbara. The weather was beautiful and sunny and their house was in a very nice neighborhood where certainly the people that lived there had a lot more money than the folks in our neighborhood. The inside of their house was decorated with much more modern and expensive furnishings than ours. It was also very clean. I wondered how Dad came to befriend someone like Doug. While my parents were visiting with Doug and Jennifer in the living room, my brothers and I stayed in a smaller room that had a television. Perhaps it was the family room or the den. Evidently, Doug and Jennifer didn't have any children. So it was just me and my three brothers in the family room. We had been trained to be good kids and to remain quiet and that's what we did. Besides, the house had such nice furniture that I didn't want to mess anything up. We were also given a lot of snacks or rather, appetizers to keep us occupied. Because my brothers and I weren't used to having appetizers, we filled our stomachs up and ate like we'd never see them again. We didn't know that dinner was going to be served soon.

After a while, Jennifer came in to see how we were doing. Jennifer was tall and very pretty, with dark hair. She also seemed very kind. She told us that dinner was going to be served soon as she gathered up all the plates from the appetizers. Soon, she came in with large white porcelain plates of food for me and my brothers. We were then given cloth napkins and utensils. The plates were filled with steak *and* chicken, potatoes and asparagus. That was the first time we ever ate asparagus. As we sat on the floor and ate our dinners off of the rectangular coffee table, my brothers and I talked about how much food there was.

"Wow, I didn't know we were going to have dinner too," I said.

"Me either," said James.

"This is a lot of food. I don't think I could eat all this," I said.

Even Luc, who could really put it away, wasn't able to finish everything off his plate. I ate as much as I could of the dinner but quickly got full. Then Jennifer came in after a while and asked us if we were finished. We looked up at her and said, "Yes." Somehow, she knew what we were thinking.

"It's okay. You don't have to eat everything," she said.

Wow. I felt relieved. I had felt so bad that I couldn't eat everything off my plate and I also felt bad that so much of the food was wasted. What was going to happen to all that food I wondered. Was she just going to throw it away? After a while, Jennifer came in with chocolate cake and ice cream. Wow! We never get dessert! This was certainly not what we were used to. Jennifer had thought of everything. Of course we couldn't eat the entire desert either.

Overall, the whole day and experience seemed strange but interesting. It felt strange to be wearing a dress again, let alone a dress that was too small for me. I constantly had to make sure my underwear wasn't showing as I sat down or got up. It felt strange to be in such a nice house with a very nice and pretty lady serving me and my brothers dinner instead of me having to make dinner or at least help. And it felt strange that I didn't have to clean up afterwards. It was as if I was back to being a little girl again.

Finally, it was time to go home. My brothers and I thanked Doug and Jennifer for their hospitality as we were leaving their house. Then, before getting into the car, Dad had Doug take a picture of us all. The sun was still out and the temperature was still nice and warm. As we drove home, I thought about my parents with Doug and Jennifer. What could they possibly talk about? Since the TV was on in the room my brothers and I were in and the adults were in a different room, I couldn't hear what they were talking about, but I would imagine Dad and Doug talking about their time in Vietnam and sharing war stories. As for Mom and Jennifer, hmmm. What would they have in common?

Mom seldom did fun things with us as a family. Usually, it would be Dad and us kids. He was the one that took us to the movies, the fair, or for Saturday morning donuts while Mom was still asleep. Of course that was in the Philippines. A lot of that stopped when we moved to the U.S. Especially now that he had four kids, instead of just two.

That winter however, my parents decided to take us kids to see the snow. We had never seen snow before and we were really excited to go. It seemed very unusual to have Mom come with us but we didn't think anything of it.

"Where are we going? I asked Dad excitedly.

"Lake Tahoe," he replied.

After driving for over three hours, we approached the higher elevations of the mountains around Lake Tahoe and soon the scenery began to change. The ground and bushes began to be dusted with the white snow. Then the ground gradually became all white and the snow began to pile high. Wow! Snow at last! And it's sunny! I had only seen pictures of it before but now, we were actually going to be able to feel it, touch it, and play in it! It was so beautiful!

Finally, Dad slowed the car down, drove it to the side of the road and parked. We all got out and my brothers and I began walking through the snow away from the car, watching the trails and track marks left behind by our feet. The air felt crisp and clean. We had never been in cool temperatures like this before but that didn't bother us. I had my green winter jacket on so that helped me stay warm. Soon, we began to run, hop, and jump in the snow. We began making snow balls and throwing them in the air and then at each other. I felt so excited and happy. Yea! We get to spend the whole day playing in the snow! Wow, what a treat this is! After only about an hour though, Dad called us to come back to the car. What? Already?

Mom was already in the car or did she ever get out? I was too busy having fun playing in the snow that I really didn't notice if Mom had gotten out or not. I figured that we were just going to go to another spot or area or perhaps someone had to use the bathroom. So we all piled back into the car and took off. Soon, we began to approach some big buildings.

"Where are we going?" I asked.

"We go inside now. When we go inside, you have to stay in room with games. Kids can't go in the casino so you have to stay in room, okay?" Mom instructed.

"Are we going to go back out in the snow later?"

"No," Dad said reluctantly.

I couldn't believe it. After only one hour?! They told us we were going to the snow! They said nothing about going to the casino or playing 21. I thought we were going to play out in the snow all day! I quickly figured out that that was just a ploy. Mom wanted to gamble and she used the guise of taking us to see the snow. I was so angry!

After parking the car, we all walked inside the casino. It was dark inside and the air was filled with cigarette smoke. There were people sitting at slot machines and you could see the many colored lights and hear the beeps, rings, and chimes coming from the slot machines. Dad led us to the game room where other kids were already playing some of the video games, then he left. We didn't know where he went or where Mom was once we were in the game room. I had never been in a casino before and I thought I might find it interesting but since we had to be confined to the game room, it wasn't much fun at all. At least not for me. Besides, I was so angry with Mom. It was just like her to be selfish and only think of herself.

The game room was small, dark, and noisy with all the kids playing the various games. Dad gave us a few quarters but I didn't play any of the games. I felt awkward and out of place. I had never played any games before and was so shy that if any of the kids looked at me, I would quickly look away. I also had to help watch Dennis who liked to roam around. A few times, he walked out of the room and we had to go after him. So I just mainly watched the other kids in amazement. They seemed so confident and knew what they were doing. After a while, I gave my quarters to James who played a few games. But I knew that he too was disappointed that we couldn't stay out in the snow longer.

# 9 The Struggle for Identity

The first school I attended in Merced was at the junior high school where I was in the sixth grade. At the time, there weren't very many Asian Americans living in Merced and so a few times, I was teased for being Asian. I would hear kids say, "Why don't you go back to where you came from," as I walked by. Or they would try to mimic talking in Chinese. They would also make reference to my eyes. I never really let those kids bother me because I didn't understand why they were teasing me. I was used to being a minority because that was how it was living on Clark Air Base. So it seemed very strange to me that they would behave that way.

They also teased me about my name and would say it in a condescending way and then giggle. Because of that, I grew to not like my name. I wanted to be normal like the other kids. Also, my two younger brothers had American names so I began to wonder why I wasn't given an American name. I asked my parents why I wasn't given an American name but received no answer. My younger brother James had a Vietnamese name listed on his birth certificate but around the house, we would call him James. Later, as an adult, he legally changed his name to the American name. When my youngest brother Dennis was born, Dad stepped in and insisted that he was going to have an American name and not have a Vietnamese name at all. I was glad that Dad did that because if it were left up to Mom, she would have given Dennis a Vietnamese name as well, which I thought would make it difficult for him because we didn't live in Vietnam but lived in the U.S.

One day, I asked Mom what my name meant in Vietnamese. Perhaps being teased at school prompted that question.

There had to be a reason why she named me the way she did. She said it was difficult to explain in English but that it was a very good name. It meant that the person who had that name was a very moral person, even though she didn't use the word "moral". She explained that that person was a very good person and always did the right thing. After hearing that explanation, I immediately felt angry. I couldn't believe it! I wanted to hear that it meant something beautiful like a flower or something else that represented beauty but no! Mom *had* to give me a name that required me to be perfect and to not have any fun. I felt that she chose that name with the intention of enforcing the restrictive life that she wanted for me, which I certainly felt. Now, knowing the meaning actually made me feel worse about my name. Not only was I teased at school about it but I also couldn't completely explain what it meant if someone were to ask me. And instead of being able to say that it meant something beautiful, it had to do with character. I wasn't even a teenager yet and had already been through so much that I didn't feel I needed any more character building experiences. Yet, the lessons would continue for much longer.

As I got older however, the kids began to find uniqueness in it. It was mostly the girls that would compliment me and say, "That's pretty," or "that's different." In those moments, it seemed to soften the contempt I had for my name but it wasn't enough. As an adult, as I kept meeting more and more Asian Americans who had American names, I began to think about changing my name—but to what? I also began to wonder what was wrong with me because they typically changed their name when they first came to the U.S. Sometimes their parents did it for them when they were still minors.

Then, because more Vietnamese were coming to the U.S., on rare occasions, I would hear someone say, "Oh I have a friend who has that name," or "I know someone who has that name." Then they would tell me that they liked that name. I would think, *That's nice that you like it but I don't.* So I would start dreaming of changing my name but something always held me back. I'd always assumed it was because I wanted to show respect for Mom but when she died, I still couldn't do it. I was an adult now and could do whatever I wanted so what was it that was holding me back? People did it all the time. I would hear about how some of the Europeans, when first coming to America, would alter their names to make life easier for them. There seemed to be this force that was keeping me down so that I would stay stuck and so that I couldn't grow or move. They say that change is hard and as much as I didn't like my name, that was certainly the case with me.

There actually weren't very many African Americans living in Merced at the time either. Merced was in the middle of a large agricultural valley that used to be a desert, so there were a lot of ranchers and farmers. There were also a lot of Mexicans that lived in the area, and most of them would form groups called cholos in school. Often, when people asked me where I'm from and where I grew up, I would tell them that I grew up in a "Hick" town because of the predominantly Caucasian American population that lived there. Interestingly, it was the Mexican kids that teased me the most. There was also this one African American girl who threatened to beat me up, and I had no idea why. I didn't know who she was, nor did I have any classes with her. Therefore, I couldn't have done anything to elicit any violence from her. I just wasn't that type of kid who would bring attention to myself. I just wanted to stay out of trouble and out of the spotlight because I received enough punishment from Mom at home. I also didn't have a lot of confidence in myself so didn't feel I could speak up like the other kids did. So this girl just came up to me one day during class changes and said, "I'm going to beat you up! Meet me after school because I'm going to beat you up." I just shrugged her off and kept going to my next class. I was scared but didn't show it and told one of my classmates, who asked me why that girl wanted to beat me up. I told her that I didn't know why. When the school day ended, I was nervous and watched for the girl to show up. But she never did. I breathed a deep sigh of relief. Thankfully, I never saw her again.

## School - A Refuge From Home

Yet despite being teased a few times for being Asian, I still preferred to be at school rather than at home. School at least gave me a break from Mom who would beat me if I was at home. I would actually tell my friends at school that I liked school. Interestingly, the friends I made at school were from all different ethnic backgrounds. One was a cute petite blond girl named Sherry who wore braces. Another was Susan, who was Mexican American and then there was Lori, who was African American and who later became my best friend. One day, when we were hanging out with each other during recess, we noticed how each of us represented a different racial group and we thought it was pretty cool.

I wasn't a very athletic kid but the one sport I did enjoy during junior high was tether ball. Despite my petite frame, I was actually pretty good at it. I was basically average with all the other sports in PE and was afraid to catch the balls when it came to playing soft ball. This was because once, when my brother James and I were practicing catch with baseball mitts, I was hit in the head with a hardened pomegranate. Instead of practicing with a real baseball or softball, we were throwing a pomegranate back and forth. For some reason, we decided to use the pomegranate because it was hard and stiff. It had gotten hard because its skin had gotten dry and lost its moisture; however, on the inside the seeds and juice remained intact.

When James threw it at me and I missed catching it, the heavy fruit hit me straight on my forehead. He threw it pretty fast, which made the pomegranate burst open and some of the seeds splattered with its juice. Though it was quite painful, I held back the tears. I didn't want to cry because I didn't want to be teased. I leaned forward and held my head with my hand and let out a yell. As James came over to see if I was okay, he saw red liquid dripping down my forehead and soaking my hands, so he thought it was blood. I saw that he was concerned so I exaggerated the pain, until I finally released my hand from my forehead and said, "Gotcha!" Even though we practiced for a little while longer, after that experience, I was afraid to catch baseballs or softballs. So whenever I was placed out in the field for a baseball game for PE or later, with friends, I would get really nervous and made sure I would find a position where I wouldn't have to catch the ball.

I also once won a blue ribbon during an athletic fair day at school in the seventh grade. This was when each student had to go around participating in different sports activities. The ribbon I won was for shooting a basketball into the basketball hoop. I really wasn't that good at basketball and didn't play it that much. It just so happened that day that I got the ball into the hoop on the first try with a granny shot. I was surprised as were the other kids, but they cheered for me after they saw the ball go into the hoop.

Since I had so many responsibilities at home and had such low self-esteem, I never considered trying out for any after school activities or sports. Even if I did feel half-way decent about myself, I knew my parents wouldn't let me because of the duties and responsibilities at home and of course, because I had to work at the restaurant. Perhaps I *could* have been good at sports but it never occurred to me to try. After all, I was a girl and there was a clear distinction between how a girl should behave and what a girl could or couldn't do in contrast to what a boy could or couldn't do.

For example, Dad would take James to play golf, or to go fishing or hunting. James would get BB guns for Christmas and over time, he would get hunting rifles or a shotgun. There were several rifles and shotguns around the house but I was never allowed to even target shoot. James allowed me to hold the rifle every now and then but because we weren't in an area where it was safe for me to pull the trigger, I didn't. I actually didn't know that Dad would take James golfing until we were adults. James loved to play golf, which I didn't know until we were talking one day. He relayed how Dad would take him golfing. When I heard that, I instantly became angry. So that's where they would go! It seemed they were always gone somewhere and I wouldn't know where they were. It wasn't so much I didn't know where they were, because I was used to that. It made me angry because I was always stuck at home, like a prisoner, even though that's all I knew. And I would be stuck at home with Mom who would take advantage of venting out her anger on me.

Over time, Dennis also was allowed to have BB guns and shotguns. However, he wasn't as level-headed and cautious as James was. Once, he accidentally fired off a BB gun in the backyard, which hit an object in our neighbor's backyard where one of their children was playing. Dennis got in big trouble for that and was not allowed to use a BB gun or shotgun for several weeks.

Certainly, the way my parents treated me made an impact on how my brothers viewed and treated me. So they began to imitate my parents' behavior. Looking back, I couldn't blame them. That was all they knew. When I was 16 and returned home from living in foster homes, Dad went to work up in Alaska. He was no longer in the military but worked as a Civil Engineer at the Naval Air Station on Adak Island, part of the Aleutian Islands archipelago. With Dad gone and Mom not home very often either, I would ask James to go with him fishing or hunting. But he refused.

"You might scream," he would say.

"Why would I scream?" I would ask.

"I don't know. Because you're a girl."

"So, just because I'm a girl doesn't mean I'll scream. I can be quiet."

"No, I don't want to risk it."

Even though I did my best to keep the house clean, having three growing brothers made it challenging. My brothers' room always stank and was messy and the living room furniture began to show wear and tear. Despite keeping my room pretty neat, Dad would always say, "You sure are sloppy for a girl." I heard that time and time again and would think, *I didn't know a girl was supposed to be neat.* I didn't know what more I could have done or what more he wanted. My room was always cleaner than my brothers. It didn't stink and I never had clothes just lying around in the bedroom. It just seemed that no matter what I did, it wasn't good enough. Perhaps it didn't look like a military dorm but even if it did, somehow he would still find something wrong.

As time went on, Dad was becoming more stressed out about the responsibility of providing financially for the family. The job he had gotten with the County as a Home Inspector didn't pay as much as when he was still in the Air Force. He also became less and less affectionate with me. When I was younger, he would tickle me until I couldn't stand it anymore but by the time I turned 12, he stopped. I guess it was because I became too strong and could fight him off much more easily.

Even though I didn't think I could do well in sports, I did love music and wanted to learn to play an instrument. When I asked Dad about learning to play an instrument, he would reply sternly, "Who's going to pay for it?" Not being able to learn to play an instrument made me feel sad. I couldn't understand how we went from living so well in the Philippines to being so poor in the U.S.

Although I would ask Dad for certain things like wanting to play an instrument, I would never have the courage to ask Mom for anything. That's because I was afraid that she would get angry and also because I knew the answer would be "no" from her, no matter what. At least with Dad, I had a chance, or so I thought. But the lack of money for things became more apparent as I saw Dad grow increasingly frustrated. I didn't realize that Mom's gambling was causing some of the frustration and part of the reason why we didn't have money for clothes or other things we needed.

I also didn't realize how tough things were getting until Mom began to bring home food from her friends. She would bring home boxes of cereal, crackers, and other things from her friends that their kids didn't like. Sometimes, they were items that had already been opened. My brothers and I didn't mind getting those things because sometimes, we would get foods we normally wouldn't get like Cocoa Puffs and Lucky Charms cereal. One time though, I went to eat some Cocoa Puffs for breakfast. I poured the cereal into a bowl, added some milk in it and began eating the cereal. Suddenly, I tasted something bitter and smelled something that didn't seem right. I looked down into the bowl and saw tiny dark bugs, crawling all over the cereal. I quickly spit the cereal I had in my mouth back into the bowl. I was disgusted. When I told Mom about the bugs in the cereal, she stopped bringing food home from her friends.

## My Best Friend

When I initially met Lori in sixth grade, I didn't actually hang out with her a lot. I knew of her but we didn't talk or do much together in school. Then in seventh grade, we had a Science class together and became science partners. Lori and I got along very well and we would talk about everything that was going on in our lives. I was so impressed with Lori's conduct because she wasn't like other kids or girls in school. For example, there was a rumor going around about our Science teacher. The other girls in the class and some outside of class would talk about how our Science teacher was weird and how he would look down girls' tops. They would giggle as they relayed this story. I would mention to the girls that he was married and they would say, "So. He still does it." When I mentioned what I had heard to Lori though, she would say, "Well, we don't know if that's true or not. He seems like a nice man and I haven't seen him do anything like that." Her reply really surprised me. I expected her to go along with the other girls but she didn't buy into it. This actually confirmed what I've been observing about him as well. Ever since I heard the rumor, I would watch to see if he indeed would look down female student's tops and I never saw him do anything like that.

Because Lori lived in the same neighborhood as me, in fact her house was only one street over from where I lived, we began to walk to and from school together. As we walked, we would talk about our home life and all the responsibilities we had at home. I would tell her how Mom treated me and Lori would relate to me about her circumstances, how her father and mother divorced many years ago when she was younger and how her two younger sisters were from a different father. She shared too how her father wasn't in her life very much, that he communicates with her perhaps once every several years, and how her mother would have different boyfriends.

Lori would also share with me what she was learning from her weekly Bible studies and how her mother didn't force her to have the studies but rather, let her decide whether she wanted to study or not. I was surprised to hear that her mom actually gave her the option to choose to do something or not. How Lori's mom treated her, which was so different than how Mom treated me, made me more receptive towards hearing what Lori had to say about the things she was learning from her weekly Bible studies. Even though Mom had told me that the Catholic Church was the only true religion. I guess it didn't matter what Mom said anymore because I had lost all respect for her. I couldn't believe the things she told me because I felt that what she said was different from what she did.

Mom would tell me how she went to Catholic school as a girl and had to get up very early in the morning to pray. They had to pray several times a day. At one point, she asked if I wanted to be a nun. She explained that it would be a very good thing to be. I was so offended by the question but couldn't show it. Although I didn't know much about sex except what I learned in school, I knew that nuns couldn't have sex and were to remain celibate. It wasn't just about the celibacy that I was offended by. It was also, as it appeared to me, that they had to live a very austere and structured life. I felt my life was already restrictive and it didn't feel good. Why would I want to be a nun? How dare she put that in my head! By her asking me that, I felt that it was like rubbing salt into a wound. Nevertheless, I would just calmly reply, "No. I don't."

Then I thought again how hypocritical it was for her to ask me to become a nun when she herself had a baby at 15. Perhaps she wanted to save me from having to go through what she did but I already knew I wasn't going to have a baby at that age. It just wasn't going to happen.

When I observed how Mom treated me, I wondered how she could have so many friends. Sometimes I would hear her complain about this friend or that friend and about the conflict or arguments they would have. Still, she obviously knew how to reconcile their conflicts to resume their friendship. I did notice though that whenever we had company over, Mom was a different person. She would be very friendly and hospitable, even laughing and smiling. I would often think, *Boy if they only knew*. After a while, I concluded that Mom was two faced. So, how could I listen to and believe her when she would tell me things and why shouldn't I listen to anyone else?

Lori and I eventually became best friends. There wasn't anything I couldn't share with her and we would talk on the phone almost every day. She was the one person that not only believed me but also understood what I was going through. Even though her mom wasn't abusive like mine, she did have a lot of responsibilities put on her as well, being the oldest of three daughters. Lori's sister Summer was two years younger than her and actually was a big help to Lori, yet they had very different personalities and the majority of responsibilities still fell on Lori. Then there was Jasmine who was the youngest and who was closer to my youngest brother Dennis's age.

Lori also kept me in check and helped me stay on the straight and narrow path. It wasn't always what she said but how she conducted herself. She was a great example of what I knew to be a good person in the world. One morning, when she came by to pick me up on the way to school, I had stormed out of the house, cursing under my breath and calling Mom a "Bitch". Even before school, Mom had managed to get angry at me and criticize me so I became angry and upset at her. Of course I couldn't say anything back to her in the house so as I walked out of the house, I slammed the door behind me and cursed at her. When Lori heard me, she said, "Wow Eden, I've never heard you talk like that before."

"Well, she made me mad," I replied. I rarely ever cursed because we weren't allowed to even though Luc did all the time. Though Lori didn't have to tell me that it was wrong to curse, I already knew. I also knew that if I was to be friends with Lori, I would have to keep my anger towards Mom and my language in check. Not because I was afraid I would lose her as a friend, it was because I respected her. I never heard her curse or get angry or upset at anyone. Even though one of her so-called friends began teasing her for studying the Bible, she wouldn't say anything back at them or retaliate. She would just turn the other cheek and walk away. As I watched how Lori would respond and behave, I became more impressed with her and my respect for her grew.

# 10 No Tips From the "Family" Business

My parents' first business venture was a small Asian Grocery store located in a small shopping center. One of the stores next to ours sold auto parts. My parents taught me how to use the cash register and stock the merchandise on the shelves, basically run the whole store, and I would work there on the weekends by myself. I was simply dropped off and left alone, with no idea where my parents were. My brothers were either at home or with my parents. At times, I would overhear the other store owners making fun of our store. I never told my parents though, what I would hear.

I wasn't crazy about working at the store but knew there was nothing I could do about it. It was just a fact of life. I don't even know if I had any thoughts of being with friends or doing what most other 11-year-old kids would do since I had no idea what other kids my age did after school or on weekends. I really didn't have any friends from school that I could associate with since I had to work at the store on the weekends, then during the week, I had the responsibility of running the whole house.

One time, I was sick with the flu. I found out that my parents were taking a trip to San Francisco to purchase more merchandise for the store. I really wanted to go with them since I had never been to a big city before. Instead, they took James, and I was left to run the store. I felt so dejected but there was no sense in complaining or resisting. If I did, I would get a beating. When we arrived at the store, my parents set up a cot in the back room that was separated by the main area of the store with just a curtain. I would lie on the cot and try to rest but it was difficult to do because every time the front door opened, I would have to slowly muster as much energy as I could to get up and walk to the front of the store, and ring up the customers. Looking back, I don't know how I had managed to even function with the shivers, chills, high fever, body aches and extreme fatigue I was experiencing. When my parents returned from San Francisco, they unloaded the merchandise in the back room then took me home. There were no "Thank You's" or asking of how I was feeling.

## A Taste of Love

That same year, Mom and Dad were suddenly placed in the hospital at the same time for several days. We didn't know why they were in the hospital. Neither one of my parents told us the reason. Later, we found out that Mom had heart surgery and one of her kidneys removed but for what reason, we weren't told. Dad had to have surgery for stomach ulcers.

Several of Dad's coworkers and a family from church came and took turns watching us kids. First, it was the Warner family from church. Mrs. Warner came all the way from Atwater and picked us up one Saturday to take us to the commissary to go grocery shopping. Since I was the one that did all the cooking, she relied on me to pick out the groceries for us.

As she pushed the shopping cart through the commissary, she would ask me what we needed. I felt so much like an adult but wasn't used to being asked what I wanted or would like. I didn't want her to spend too much money on us so I made sure we only got the necessities. When she would ask if we wanted certain items that our parents wouldn't normally get for us, I would reply, "No, that's okay. We don't need that." Yet, she assured me that if we wanted it, it would be okay. My brothers on the other hand were so excited about her generosity and willingness to get us almost whatever we wanted that they would ask for certain things we normally wouldn't get from our parents. I would almost scold them for being so impolite; however, Mrs. Warner kept saying, "It's okay. If you want that, we will get it."

I had never been around someone who was so kind and generous, who treated me like a real person and not like a slave or a child whose only purpose for existence was to be a servant to her family. Mrs. Warner didn't stay the night at our house but she did have us spend the night at her house. Mrs. Warner and her husband had three children of their own but somehow, they were able to accommodate my three brothers and me.

The next day, Sunday, we went to church and then after church, we came back to their house and got to swim in their above ground swimming pool. As I watched her children, who were older than my brothers and me, swim and play around in the pool, I noticed how they were laughing, talking, playing, and just having a great time. It was natural for them to be able to express themselves since this was their home and pool of course. However, beyond them being comfortable in their own home environment, I noticed they had no inhibitions, only confidence to express themselves. It was as if my brothers and I weren't even there. While I did get in the pool, I was self conscious, not only because this wasn't my home and that I didn't know these kids very well, but because I wasn't used to expressing myself. As I watched her two sons and daughter, I wished I were able to express myself and just have fun as they did. I also wished Mrs. Warner were my mother. I didn't know it at the time but I felt there was a lot of love in the family.

After we finished swimming, Mrs. Warner took my brothers and me back home to our house. After she left, a couple from Dad's office came to stay with us, Ted and Debbie. They seemed like a very happy couple, always whispering to each other and laughing. They were also very affectionate with each other. Ted would cook for us and even made chicken cooked in Coke one night. He explained that the chicken would absorb the Coke as I watched him cook. He was right, the chicken tasted sweet.

Even though my parents were strict, we often had little to no supervision. So we were left to fend for ourselves with me taking care of the household. Therefore, it was quite normal for us to help ourselves to the food in the refrigerator. Every now and then, they would buy candy or special snacks like Ding Dongs or Ho Ho's. Mom would get angry at us for getting into the snacks. We couldn't help it. We knew we weren't supposed to eat the snacks or candy since we didn't have much money and those were only given to us at special times. But with Dad working and going to school in the evenings and Mom almost never home, how would she know who took them?

However, when Ted and Debbie stayed with us, they ran a tight ship. Perhaps that's how my parents would have been if they had been home more. One day, I went into the refrigerator and took an apple out of the vegetable/fruit bin and started to eat it. Debbie noticed I had taken an apple without permission and asked, "Do your parents let you get whatever you want out of the refrigerator without asking?"

"Yes," I replied as nonchalantly as I could. How silly I thought. I've been cooking for my entire family and was more the mom of the house than my own mother and to think that I had to ask for an apple? Thankfully, Debbie didn't challenge it any further.

A few days before my parents were to come home from the hospital, Uncle George, who really wasn't our uncle, and who was Dad's friend from the Air Force, came by to help get the house prepared for my parents' arrival. Uncle George told me to change the sheets of my parents' bed. I had never made my parents' bed before, which was a lot bigger than mine and I never had any "formal" training in making a bed. I just knew the fitted sheet went on the mattress and the loose sheet went before the blanket.

As Uncle George watched me make the bed, he realized that I wasn't making it exactly military style so he came over to assist me.

"Didn't your parents show you how to make a bed?" he asked.

"No," I replied.

"Well, let me show you." he said in a frustrated tone. So he showed me how to tuck the corners in neatly and showed me how to fold Dad's T-shirts so they would look nice and square. No, my parents didn't teach me those details. I had already been doing the laundry, the cooking, and cleaning of the rest of the house but wasn't taught to make a bed or fold T-shirts the way Uncle George showed me. I knew he was Dad's friend and cared about my parents' health but why did I have to be the one responsible for getting the house ready? What about my brothers? I'm only 11 and didn't I matter? I wasn't asking to go outside to be with friends and play, since I had no concept of having friends. I just wanted some relief from all the pressure and responsibilities of the household. For once, it would be nice for an adult to do some chores around the house without my help. Thankfully, while my parents were in the hospital I didn't have to work at the Asian store.

After the one year lease with the Asian store was over, my parents bought a Chinese and French restaurant from some friends of theirs. It was called the Mekong Restaurant after the longest river that ran throughout Southeast Asia. My parents' friends were a Vietnamese family who had a daughter that was a year older than me named Lynn. Lynn seemed to enjoy her job of waiting on tables and so I thought I would enjoy it also, but I didn't. After getting settled into the routine of working at my parents' restaurant, I realized that what I really wanted was to be normal like the other kids at school who didn't have to work at a restaurant. I wanted to have friends and to do things with them.

The Phan's also had a daughter about James's age named Amy, who helped at the restaurant with Lynn, and two younger boys about ages six and four. The boys were too young to help out so it was mainly Lynn and Amy. Mrs. Phan would do most of the cooking with Mr. Phan's help. As a family, they actually ran the restaurant. This observation didn't seem that significant until my parents took it over.

On opening day, the restaurant became filled and noisy with curious customers wanting to see if the food would be any better than when it was owned by the Phan's. Lynn had trained me to wait on the tables but there was no way I could be prepared for the onslaught of customers that came in. Furthermore, there was no way Mom could keep up with the orders that came in either, even though she had a cook to help her. Mom had cooked for people before when we would have parties or gatherings at our house but she had no experience running a restaurant or cooking for the numbers of customers that were coming in.

So the Phan's were called in to help. Since Mr. and Mrs. Phan helped with much of the cooking, the food essentially hadn't changed. I would hear the customers commenting on how it wasn't any different. It was a shame that they weren't able to really distinguish the difference in how the dishes were prepared or tasted because I actually thought Mom was a better cook than Mr. or Mrs. Phan. However, the Phan's sold the restaurant because they wanted to open up another restaurant in a bigger town. To me, they seemed to have a better grasp and understanding of what it took to run a restaurant. The Phan's actually worked as a family to run the business. My parents just simply wanted to be the owners. I quickly learned that you just can't simply buy a restaurant and merely become owners. You have to work at it, at least for a while, but Dad had a full-time job and went to school during some of the evenings. If he wasn't in school, then he would somehow disappear like my brothers and I wouldn't know where he was. I didn't think to ever ask where he was either because that was just how things were.

After some time, Mom was able to keep up with the orders and I was able to keep up with my duties at the restaurant of being hostess, waitress, bus boy, cashier, and even dishwasher. Behind the cash register counter, there were shelves where the drinking glasses and mugs were stored and where I would wash them in a sink in front of the order window. There was a soda fountain and ice machine for drink orders, and pitchers for water, as well as a small refrigerator for the chilled wine and alcoholic beverages. Even though I was only 12, I served alcoholic beverages, which was illegal, but I didn't know that. And nobody ever protested or felt it necessary to file a report. Since Lynn, who was 13, could serve alcohol then my parents figured it was okay for me to serve it too.

Even though I performed all those duties, I was never allowed to keep any of the tips. I was to place them in a small tin pail underneath the counter. I never thought of taking any of the tips, even when there was nobody around to watch me. Where could I go to spend the money? Besides, I just knew that somehow, Mom would catch me if I did. She just had this innate ability to know if I was lying or if I had done something wrong, which wasn't very often because of that very reason.

Eventually, Mom cooked less and less and wouldn't even come to the restaurant. She would come if it was a busy time or had to do paper work, but other than that, the hired cook, an older Vietnamese woman, did all the cooking. What a shame because Mom was a much better cook. I believed that if Mom did more of the cooking, we would have more customers and business would be better. To me, it seemed really simple. You serve good food, provide good customer service, then more people would come because they would like the food and want to come back, and then they would also tell their friends. Therefore, your business would increase. I couldn't understand why my parents didn't seem to get that. With the food being cooked by mostly the hired cook, that wasn't going to happen.

I also began to wonder why I didn't enjoy working at the restaurant like Lynn did. She was more confident and outgoing than I was and not afraid to express herself. And she seemed pretty happy with working at the restaurant. Why was that? As I studied and observed her and her family, I began to notice several differences in the Phan's family dynamics compared to my family's and how our families ran the restaurant differently. First of all, I noticed that both Mr. and Mrs. Phan worked at the restaurant and they had two girls that worked as well. I learned that Lynn got to keep the tips and she seemed to have more freedom than I did. Even though at times, when my family was visiting the Phan's at their home, I would see Mrs. Phan getting on Linda about something (they would speak in Vietnamese so I couldn't understand what they were saying but I could tell Linda was being told to do something), Linda would always reply in a respectful manner. She never seemed to let what Mrs. Phan said bother her and she never indicated that her mother or father ever hit her. As in my own family, I got the sense that Mrs. Phan had more say and power in the family; however, it wasn't like Mom. And Mr. Phan was no coward like Dad and had a lot to say about the family business since he worked at the restaurant also. They just seemed to have more business savvy and really knew what it took to run a business.

Lynn also liked to have fun and seemed to be happy with her family. She made friends easily and was always looking forward to the next adventure. So she didn't have time for details. One Christmas, when our family was invited over to the Phan's, after dinner was over, Lynn had to wash the dishes. The rest of the family went on to the living room to start opening gifts. I went to help Lynn with the dishes because I just knew it would be expected of me. You could hear the wrapping papers being opened and the younger kids, mainly Lynn's younger brothers and my youngest brother getting all excited. Lynn didn't want to miss out on the fun of opening gifts so she hurriedly rinsed the dishes with a brush and put them on the dish bin to dry without using soap. As I watched her, I couldn't believe what I was seeing.

"You're not using soap?" I asked astonished but calmly.

"No," she replied, as she continued to wash the dishes hurriedly.

"How come you're not using soap?" I asked again in disbelief.

"It doesn't really matter. We're just going to use them again," she said, while attempting to ignore her feelings of embarrassment.

The site of her washing the dishes without soap and not even with hot water seemed so disgusting to me and made me nauseous. *How long have they been doing this?* I wondered. Later, I told Dad about how Linda didn't use soap or hot water to wash the dishes. He said, "You think that's bad. I knew this family who would just lick their plates clean and then turn their plates over and leave them on the table," as he demonstrated with his hands.

"Ewe! That's gross!" I exclaimed.

Certainly, the stereotype of Asian people being very clean was not true. I had been in many of Mom's friend's homes, including the Phan's where the homes weren't kept as clean as ours, and that was with only me cleaning it. Having three growing brothers and two dogs didn't help the situation so it wasn't perfect but Mom certainly had a higher standard of cleanliness than some of her other friends. Also, I was used to having a clean home because in the Philippines, we had maids that always kept the house immaculate.

As for Christmas, yes opening gifts on Christmas day was exciting for me but never *that* exciting. At least not after we had moved to the U.S. That was because I began to notice that my brothers always got more gifts and bigger things for Christmas than I did. I also noticed that my parents would ask my brothers what they wanted for Christmas but they wouldn't ask me. So, for the most part, my brothers would get what they wanted. They would get BB guns or shotguns, or other things that they had wanted. James and Dennis would get so excited. For me though, it would be clothes and things that I actually needed. Many times, I would feel sad and disappointed as I opened my gifts to see that it was a sweater or socks or something else that I had needed during the school year but my parents had waited until Christmas to give me. Whereas my brothers received things they could play with or have fun with. The only toy I ever received after moving to the U.S. was a large sized teddy bear, about 18" tall, that I kept for years into my adulthood because it was the only toy I had to remind me of my youth. But eventually, Mr. Nickerbocker, as I had named the teddy bear and which was also the name of the toy company as advertised on the tag, was donated.

Needless to say, I would often fake a smile and pretend I was happy when Dad took our pictures by the Christmas tree, but underneath it all, I wanted to cry. Did my parents not think that I would catch on and not see what was going on? Or was that their way again of ensuring that I knew I was just a second class human being, not worthy of having any joy or fun in life? I felt humiliated. Clearly my brothers were more important than I was, especially my two younger ones, even though I was the one that took care of them and the house. Sadly, I doubted my brothers even noticed the difference in the type of gifts they received compared to what I received. They were too busy being excited about their own gifts and despite my observation, I never said anything to them about it or complained to my parents. I felt that it would have been hopeless to do so.

At times, when it was really slow at the restaurant, Mom would come to the restaurant and burn paper in a round metal container. She would place the metal container on one of the red plastic serving tray, the ones used to serve the dishes of food to the customers, and walk around the restaurant. I asked her why she was doing that. She said that it was to scare the evil spirits away that were keeping the customers from coming. She believed that when it was slow, it had something to do with evil spirits so burning paper would scare them off.

Mom was quite superstitious and I often thought that she was ridiculous for having them. They just didn't make sense to me. Besides, I knew that none of the moms of the other kids at school would do anything like this. I also didn't want to have anything to do with Mom's culture since she wasn't someone I respected or felt any affinity to. I guess this was one of the ways I began to start rebelling. Instead of being curious and drawn to Mom's culture, I didn't want anything to do with it. I wanted to be normal like the other kids in school.

One of the things she believed was that if I gave her flowers prior to her going out to play bingo, then that would make her lucky. So she would buy the flowers and then turn around and tell me to give them to her. This would make her lucky and at times it worked and she would win at bingo. Mom was also superstitious about black cats. Once, we were driving somewhere and a black cat ran across the street. Mom told Dad to turn around and go a different direction. Even though he didn't believe in it, Mom was insistent so he complied.

During the week, Dad would come home from work and pick us kids up, then take us to the restaurant, which was about a 15-minute drive. After he dropped us off, he went to his evening classes. Where exactly that was, I didn't know and I didn't know if it was every evening of the week or not. Often times, I just didn't know where my parents were. Mom was most likely playing Chinese cards with her friends, playing bingo or some other form of gambling, but where specifically and with whom, was never communicated to me.

## A "Rebellious" Streak

At the restaurant, I would wait on tables and then do my homework in between customers. I would also cook dinner for my younger brothers and help James with his homework. Luc was able to cook for himself by that time. Since Mom and Dad weren't around, I decided to start drinking some of the wine that was served to the customers. I figured that since Mom was always telling me that I was a bad kid, I may as well behave like one. However, since I didn't like the bitter taste of the

Burgundy wine, which was my wine of choice because of the rich color, I would add sugar and ice to make it taste better.

I would also sneak a cigarette from a pack that Dad would leave lying around. I would smoke it at one of the smaller tables that was against a wall and behind a partition where nobody could see me, unless it was someone coming in through the front door. It wasn't something I did on a daily basis, just every once in a while. This was before cigarette smoking was banned from inside restaurants. I would suck and pull on the cigarette and then blow out the smoke. I thought I was so cool. Now I'll show my parents what a bad kid *really* does! However, I wouldn't dare smoke a cigarette in front of them. I knew better than that. I also knew that cigarette smoking wasn't good for you.

One day at school during recess, I was sitting on the grass with several of my classmates. There were about four or five of us all sitting in a circle and I began to brag about how I had started smoking. I thought they would think I was cool. Instead, they told me how bad it was for me. Susan said, "You know that smoking cigarettes is bad for you don't you?" I replied embarrassed, "Yes, I know." I was disappointed and surprised. That was the last thing I expected my friends to say to me. What was wrong with them!? It seemed even my own friends wouldn't let me do anything wrong!

Well, I guess that's what happens when you hang out with nerdy, and "A" student friends. I look back and realized that I actually had positive peer pressure. Thankfully I did because after that, I did stop "smoking". After seeing movies with characters who were smoking for the first time, I realized that I hadn't really been smoking. The people that were really inhaling the cigarette smoke started to gag and cough. I thought that's what I had done but since I didn't gag or get sick, I concluded that I hadn't really been smoking. I also learned that as soon as someone takes their first puff of a cigarette, they had a very high chance of becoming addicted. I was thankful that I really didn't know what I was doing. I wondered if someone up above was looking after me.

Over the years Mom would get on Dad for smoking, constantly telling him he needed to stop. He would stop, for a while, but when things got stressful, he would start smoking again. Finally, he stopped smoking for good.

On Friday evenings and during the weekend when it was busier, they had another waitress help me with serving the customers. The waitress was an 18 year old, half Japanese and half African American girl named Tangela, which she told me meant Tangerine in Japanese. Even she wasn't able to keep all the tips when she worked. She was only allowed to take half the tips during the shifts that she worked.

One weekday evening when Mom happened to be at the restaurant, it got really busy. A large group of people came in after an event and soon the restaurant became packed. I called Tangela to come in to help but she said she was sick with the flu. I felt so overwhelmed and my heart raced as I heard and saw the people keep coming in through the front door, which had a bell on it. They began to fill up almost all the tables in the restaurant. I tried my best to wait on all the tables but I just couldn't keep up. Fortunately, most of the customers were understanding since they saw that I was the only one there doing everything. I was hosting and seating them, taking their orders, bringing their drinks, which included giving them water first, serving their dishes, running and giving them their bill that came with a fortune cookie for each person at the table, and finally, running the cash register. If I didn't have so many people to still wait on, I would have started bussing the tables but there was no time to bus tables yet.

Mom told me to call Tangela again. After calling Tangela several times throughout the evening, she finally came in to help. The people had began coming in at around 5 PM and by the time Tangela got there, it was after 8 PM. By that time, most of the tables had been served and there were only a few tables left that needed their orders taken. After things settled down, Tangela helped with bussing some of the tables and then decided to leave. However, before she left, she decided to take half the tips that had been collected throughout the evening. The tip can had tips from the tables that I had waited on prior to her coming to the restaurant. She was only at the restaurant for maybe one hour and she somehow felt entitled to take more than her share of the tips. I didn't quite feel that it was fair so I immediately informed Mom. From the order window, Mom gestured and whispered to me to tell Tangela, who had her back turned away from the window, not to take half the tips. However, I was afraid to tell Tangela that because she was older than me, which made Mom angry. With a frown on her face, she kept whispering and telling me to stop Tangela, but I just couldn't do it. Then I became angry at Mom for making me do her dirty work. Why couldn't she tell Tangela herself?

After that event, I again noticed that I was doing all the work in the restaurant and my brothers Luc and James didn't have to do anything. I even had to clean the one bathroom in the restaurant. So once again, I began to complain to my parents and finally, they had Luc wash the bigger dishes, like the dinner plates and the pots and pans. Prior to that, the cook had washed those dishes. They also had him and James begin bussing the tables. I realized that if I hadn't said anything, my parents would have continued to let me do everything.

# 11 Words a Child Should Never Hear

Even though Mom was gone a lot, I didn't mind. Although I was basically the surrogate mother and had a lot of responsibilities, at least I would have some peace and wasn't being verbally, emotionally, and physically abused when she wasn't home. If she were home, she would always find some reason to beat me and punish me. There was nothing I could do to please her and there was no getting around it. And often times, there was nobody else but her and me at home. When James asked Mom why she had it out for me, it was based on what he saw. He, my other brothers and Dad never really saw all the other times Mom had beaten me. She was clever that way. Consequently, she could just unleash her anger and say the vilest things. "You know, I could do what I want with you! Because you are the daughter and I am the mother, I can do what I want! Do you understand me?!" My brothers would be out with their friends and Dad would be at work or school. But me, I had nowhere to go.

Mom would beat me with anything she could find, a fly swatter that had a wire metal handle, wooden kitchen spoons and sometimes even a knife. She would turn the knife to its flat side but in her anger, I was afraid that one day she would accidentally or intentionally turn the knife and she would end up cutting me severely. I told Dad one day that I was afraid of Mom. He scoffed at me and said, "What are you afraid for? That's ridiculous."

Frequently, in her anger and in her beating me she would tell me that I was a terrible child for not obeying her, for giving her "black looks" or "ugly looks". I'm sure she meant dirty looks. How could I look at someone, even my mother, with love and affection when she was always beating me for no reason? How can I give and show love when it wasn't shown to me, especially to someone whom I didn't feel loved me? And I didn't understand why she kept saying I was being disobedient because I did everything she wanted me to. I can only imagine what she would do if I *really* disobeyed her. If this is what she does when I did all the cooking and cleaning, what would she do if I actually did talk back and lash back at her?

When Mom was beating me, all I could do was just curl up in a tight fetal position on the floor, tuck my head down close to my knees, and cover my head with my hands. I would block out what she was yelling at me for because most of the time it just didn't make any sense. I would also try very hard not to cry because I didn't want her to see me break down.

Mom would also corner me in the bathroom and lecture me on how bad I was. She would tell me, "When I was your age, I had to work very hard." I guess I had it easy compared to her, since I got to live in the U. S. and go to school and not have to work outside the home. She would also say that because I was a girl, I had ruined her luck. If she'd had four boys, she would be a lucky woman but I ruined that for her because I was a girl. Even the animal sign I was born under, according to Mom, made me a bad and evil person as well.

I didn't know anything about Vietnamese Astrology and almost didn't want know because I didn't want to have anything to do with Mom's culture. *After all*, I thought, *why should I? Look at how she's treating me?* She would also say things like, "You know, I should have killed you when you were a baby" or "I should have left you in the garbage can where I found you!" I finally figured out at around twelve that there was something not quite right about Mom. I realized that she was jealous of me. How sick I thought. What mother would be jealous of her own daughter? If it was me and I had a difficult upbringing, I would want the best for my daughter. I would want things to be different for her and I would make sure she wouldn't have to go through the same things I went through. I decided right there and then that when I grew up and had children, I would *never* treat my children the way Mom treated me. I was certain there was a better way even though I didn't know what it was.

It was also around that age when Mom started telling me that Dad wasn't my real father. So now at the age of twelve, she decided that it was time I should know the truth? Was that meant to hurt me even more? "You know, your father is not really your father," she would say as she was reprimanding and lecturing me on how I was such a disobedient and bad child.

"I know," I would reply. *So what does that have to do with anything?* I thought.

It was about that time too when Dad would say to me, "You know when I got you, you were cute as a button." I guess that was his own way of telling me that I had a different father. I didn't know what a button had to do with cuteness. I would imagine a button and wondered how someone could look like a button. Oh well, at least he thought I was cute. I'm glad somebody did.

When you are constantly told these things, it's a wonder that I didn't feel good about myself. Even at the restaurant, if Mom was around, she would find a way to beat me or verbally abuse me. There were times I would go into the restroom at the restaurant when there weren't any customers and sit on the tile floor and just cry, wishing I were dead and wanting to kill myself. I was so full of anger and hate for Mom and felt nothing but misery and pain. I hated my life and I hated Mom. I wondered what I did to deserve a life like this. I didn't ask to be born and if I *had* been given a choice I would have said, "No! I do not want to be here!"

A couple of times, I would get a nail file or some other object to try and cut my wrist. I was actually too scared to use a real knife and the sight of blood made me sick. I would imagine myself bleeding on the floor and then someone finding me. Perhaps then, *someone* would pay attention to me or care about me, and perhaps they would all be sorry for how they treated me. But deep down, I didn't want to die. I wanted to live. I just wanted the suffering and pain to stop.

Reflecting back, I realized that I was being beaten every single day Mom was home. At the time it was normal for me but putting it into perspective, it was about three to five times a week and at the same time being told I was ugly, stupid, bad, and evil. The reason it wasn't seven days a week was because those were the days and nights when Mom wasn't home.

Interestingly, throughout my adult life, I would occasionally encounter women who for some reason would start yelling at me. They could be a coworker or a roommate and I would just shut down. I wouldn't be able to hear what they were saying and would have a difficult time responding to them. I would almost black out audibly and become paralyzed. Instead of sticking up for myself, I would just take the abuse and then I would get angry at myself later for not having the courage to stick up for myself or say something back. I realize now that the reason these women would yell at me is because they were frustrated with themselves or felt threatened by me for some reason. I also learned that their frustrations had nothing to do with me. It didn't happen very often but when it did, I came to realize that I reacted to them the way I reacted to Mom by just shutting down.

When I told some of my friends at school about Mom, they wouldn't believe me. "How can your mother be like that. I don't believe you." Then I would show them the red and swollen welts on my arms that were in the shape of the metal handle of the fly swatter that Mom had used to beat me that morning.

One day when my parents weren't home, I went to Sue's house, a classmate who lived in my neighborhood. I had taken a risk to leave the house since I rarely ever got to do so. I always had to stay home and make sure chores were done. My brothers were able to leave the house and go with their friends or play outside but I wasn't able to. James would go hunting or fishing with his friends, and I often wouldn't know where he was. Luc would be out playing sports on the street with his friends and Dennis would be with Mom and Dad or with James.

I really wasn't allowed to have friends either. As an adult, when I first learned of the concept of children being grounded as a form of discipline, which meant that their privileges were taken away from them and that they had to stay at home for a week or two because of some misbehavior, I realized that I was practically grounded my whole life, whether I misbehaved or not. I never thought that I was being grounded because that word was never used at home and because I didn't know any better. I just accepted it as normal in my life. However, I couldn't help but feel trapped and imprisoned. I wanted to fly and be free from this crazy family and from my crazy mother but I wasn't allowed to go anywhere.

Except on that warm and sunny day when I went to Sue's house, I saw a small window of opportunity, and so I took it. I didn't know where my parents where and when they were returning home. When I went to Sue's house, she was outside in her front yard. Sue was a slightly chubby girl, fair skinned with freckles all over her face and body. She had blondish, reddish hair that came to her shoulders and big blue eyes. We just hung out in her front yard and talked. I shared with her how badly Mom was treating me.

"I can't believe your mom would treat you like that. My Mom tells me she loves me all the time. She calls me 'sunshine'," Sue related to me.

"Wow, your mom tells you she loves you? My mom would never say that."

Soon, I saw Sue's mom open the front door to call Sue in for something, which prompted me to go home. I don't recall how long I was at Sue's house but it couldn't have been that long since I knew I wasn't supposed to be wandering around in the neighborhood that far away from home. When I arrived home, the garage door was open and so was the door to the house inside the garage. James, who was 11 at the time, was helping Dad deep clean the carpet. Dad had rented a Rug Doctor. Uh oh. I had no idea Dad was going to be cleaning the carpet and that he would be home before me.

As soon as I walked in the door, Dad began yelling at me and demanding to know where I had been. I told him that I had been at a friend's house. "Who told you, you could go to a friend's house?! Because you weren't home, your brother had to help me!" he yelled. Before I could say anything else, he began hitting and punching me. He finally knocked me down to the floor where I fell against the screen door which sprung open. I ended up laying halfway out into the garage, with my body sprawled over the threshold and on the concrete garage door step and the other half, my legs were in the house. While I was still lying on the floor, Dad began to kick me. As I tried to protect myself from his blows and position myself so I could get up, Dad had kicked me in the stomach, knocking the wind out of me. I immediately held my stomach and gasped for air. Finally, when Dad saw that I couldn't breathe, he stopped kicking me. I kept gasping until finally, I was able to take a breath. Dad yelled at me to get up, which I somehow managed to have the strength to do. I was devastated, hurt, angry, and humiliated. I was 13 and had all these adult responsibilities heaped upon me but once again, I'm being treated like a child and not shown any appreciation. I expected it from Mom but not from Dad. I got up and went to my room crying, crushed and perplexed as to why Dad would do such a thing. It seemed that Mom had turned him over to her side. What was wrong with James helping out? I know he was only 11 but *I* learned to cook and do all the chores in the house at age 10!

Dad rarely beat me but when he did, it was much more painful physically since he was a man and much stronger than Mom. It seemed that after Dad retired from the Air Force and started working as a residential construction inspector, the financial stress was really getting to him. The pay just wasn't what he was used to making and now, he had four kids to care for. Also, the increase in animosity between Mom and me didn't help the home environment either.

Up until a certain point, Dad was the reasonable, stable, and level-headed one emotionally but after having had surgery for ulcers and learning of Mom's prognosis (which was not revealed to us kids at the time), along with the financial stress and the increased anger and resentment from Mom towards me, his emotional and mental stability began to slowly erode. One time, Mom was getting on me for something and Dad tried to defend me. Mom began to turn on him and started crying and yelling at him saying, "You take her side! You don't love me!"

"That has nothing to do with it. I'm just saying you need to back off a little bit. What did she do that was so bad?" Dad implored?

"I don't care. You take her side so you don't love me! I hate you, you son of a bit (bitch)!"

"You leave my mother out of this! Stop saying that!"

"You son of a bit (bitch)!"

Of course Mom had no idea what she was saying. That was the last time Dad ever defended me. It wasn't worth it to have your wife go crazy and inflict a guilt trip on you in order to defend a daughter who wasn't really yours biologically. He'd realized that Mom's anger towards me had nothing to do with him. So Dad stormed out of the house through the garage door, slamming it behind him without saying a word. That's how Dad usually dealt with Mom when she would get angry or cause a ruckus. Taking the path of least resistance was much easier. As I saw that Dad didn't have the courage to stand up to Mom anymore, I began to lose respect for him as well. It seemed everyone was afraid of Mom.

One summer, Mom worked at a peach cannery and would bring crates of peaches home. They were very large, juicy and delicious. Aside from that and working at the restaurant, she didn't work outside the home. She was mostly gone a lot, playing Chinese cards with her friends, playing bingo, or going to a casino. She would also take trips to Las Vegas, Reno, or Tahoe to gamble. I guess that was her way of trying to bring money in for the family. I didn't realize that Mom had a gambling problem until James told me when we were adults.

I had always wondered why we didn't seem to have enough money. It just seemed like a normal thing for Mom to be gone all the time, playing Chinese cards with her girl friends. Sometimes they would come to our house and play

Chinese cards but mostly she would be gone at one of their homes. I guess that was so she wouldn't have to deal with us kids. At the time, I thought that was just what mothers did. Later, as I thought about her gambling addiction and how she squandered what Dad worked so hard for, I became angry. Instead of spending the money to buy us clothing and shoes, or anything else we needed for school, it was spent for her own selfish desires.

When I started the sixth grade and was taking Physical Education (PE), we were required to wear tennis shoes but my parents refused to buy them for me. I kept telling them that I had PE and my PE teacher required everyone to wear tennis shoes. But it kept falling on deaf ears.

One day, my parents took my brothers and me to the BX on base. We were in the shoe section and one by one, my parents bought each of my brothers a pair of tennis shoes. As I sat silently and watched my brothers trying on different pairs of tennis shoes, I tried so hard not to cry but I couldn't fight it. Tears started rolling down my face. It was as if I was watching a very sad movie. I was hurt and crushed, as if the wind had been taken out of my lungs and I became weak. I had been begging my parents to buy me a pair of tennis shoes for PE but they wouldn't and now they were buying all my brothers a pair of tennis shoes and I had to sit and watch the scene. As I sat watching, I kept hoping they would have me look for a pair of tennis shoes, but they didn't. I had already asked them several times and they kept saying I didn't need them. I don't know if it was because I was a girl or they just wanted to punish and hurt me even more. But for what, I didn't know. It wasn't because they didn't have enough money because they never said to me that they couldn't afford it. Obviously, things weren't that tight since they were able to buy each of my brothers a pair of tennis shoes. What would have been one more pair? I don't know if my parents noticed that I was silently crying or not. If they did, they didn't say anything.

Finally, in PE class our PE teacher had us line up outside for roll call. It was a hot and bright sunny day, and we were dressed in our PE shorts and top. I remember standing in line on the concrete slab where the basketball courts were, side by side with the other girls in class as the teacher walked up to each one of us. When she reached me and stood in front of me with her clipboard and pen to take roll, she looked down at my feet. I was wearing sandals, one of two pairs of shoes I owned. The other pair of shoes was for church. I was the only one wearing sandals.

"You need to get some tennis shoes," she said.

"I know," I replied as I looked down at my feet.

I felt really embarrassed but kept my mouth shut. I didn't go into telling her that I had been telling my parents all along to get me a pair of tennis shoes but they refused to. I wanted to but I couldn't. Something held me back. Maybe it was because I thought she wouldn't believe me anyway or I was just too afraid to speak up.

I went home and told my parents what happened, telling them that I was the only girl in PE class that didn't have any tennis shoes. Finally, they allowed me to get a pair of tennis shoes. It was difficult for me to understand why my parents didn't believe me. Perhaps they didn't have PE when they were growing up in Germany or Vietnam but couldn't they understand that we were living in the U.S. and that things had changed? What could possibly be going through their heads? I was baffled.

Even though I didn't have a lot of clothes to wear to school, I just accepted that fact and didn't say too much to my parents about getting more clothes for school. It was hard enough to get the tennis shoes. As it was, I only had two pairs of pants that I would alternate wearing every other day. I had a pair of yellow dittos and a pair of light blue dittos. One day, while getting some books out of my locker, a school friend asked me in front of a couple of other classmates, in an attempt to embarrass me, "How come you wear those pants all the time." I was wearing my yellow ditto pants.

I immediately replied assuredly and tersely, "Because I like them. They're my favorite pair of pants."

I had no idea where that came from but I was quite proud of myself for coming up with such a clever deflective remark that quickly. I was too embarrassed to say that my parents couldn't afford to buy me any more clothes. Evidently, I was convincing enough because she never brought it up again.

Ironically, Mom bought a sewing machine, which at first I thought she had bought for herself so she could do some sewing. She later told me that she had bought the sewing machine for me. Fortunately, I had taken a Home Economics class in the sixth grade and learned how to sew. Soon, I began to sew and make many of my own clothes through junior and high School. In high school, I would make some pretty unique outfits and I would get compliments on them. I was proud of the things that I made, especially because I knew nobody else had anything like them. Soon, I began to get requests from friends who wanted me to sew for them. I did sew a few things for them but learned from a much wiser woman that I really needed to charge more for what I was doing to make it worth my while. I soon learned that I couldn't charge people what I really wanted and have them save money. After all, part of sewing your own clothes was to save money. At least in my case it was. So eventually, I decided to stop sewing for other people. However,

I continued to sew dresses, lined suits, winter coats, and blouses, and I would also make curtains and comforters as well. People were amazed and impressed with the things that I sewed. My inspiration to create and sew these things came from my mentor and Bible teacher, Mary Jane, whom I began studying with when I was 16.

I also took Spanish in the sixth grade and thought I did pretty well in that class but for some reason I couldn't seem to get an "A". Spanish seemed pretty easy to me. All the letters were enunciated and I when it came to the tests, I always got good scores. Mrs. Silva, our Spanish teacher, was a very petite and slightly pudgy Hispanic lady. I noticed though that Mrs. Silva definitely had a favorite student or teacher's pet. She would often call on Shirley Menini even when she didn't have her hand up and Shirley almost always had the answer correct. She called on Shirley so much that her name has been ingrained in my brain for the rest of my life.

One Saturday, Mrs. Silva came to the restaurant with her husband and children. I was surprised to see that Mrs. Silva's husband was not Mexican. He was Caucasian with blond hair and blue eyes. Mrs. Silva and her husband ordered beer with their food. Then Mrs. Silva's husband ordered another beer. Then another, then another. After about the fifth beer, I could see Mrs. Silva's embarrassed look on her face. "Hun, that's enough beers," she said to her husband. *Wow, I guess teachers have issues too*, I thought. What could her husband be stressed about I wondered.

After Mom's heart surgery and the removal of one of her kidneys, one of the things she would have me do was give her massages. My brothers didn't have to give her the massages. It was always me, which made me resentful. I had grown to feel disgusted around her, like I didn't want to be near her. And yet she demanded that I give her massages. She would also have me rub a green Chinese oil that smelled like mint on her back. Once the oil was on her back, I would have to scrape her back with a coin until she had these red marks down her back. Another treatment she would have me administer was the Chinese suction cup therapy, which made me think she was really strange. I didn't understand what those treatments did or knew what they were called since she never explained them to me. I also didn't understand why I had to be the one to administer them to her instead of Dad, my older brother or one of her friends. I was certain none of the other kids at school had to do anything like this. Because these treatments seemed so strange to me, I never told anybody about them.

One day, I heard Dad say that ever since Mom came back from the hospital and from her surgery, she was not the same. The surgery Mom had on her heart and having one kidney removed had changed her personality. She had always looked at me with disdain but now her anger and hatred intensified. With the knowledge that she only had five years to live, you would think that she would want to spend as much time with her children as possible, but that was not the case with Mom. And instead of wanting the best for me, her only daughter, she intended the worst for me, and did everything she could to make my life as miserable as possible. I kept asking myself what was wrong with this picture and what was it about me that she hated so much.

It became apparent that she was just going to do what she wanted, despite having children. She behaved and lived as if she didn't have children. Besides, she had me to do everything. So, she continued to be with her friends, gamble, travel, socialize, and sing. Some of these things I didn't know she was doing until I was in my twenties and looked through some photo albums at Dad's house after Mom had passed. I saw a picture of Mom on-stage, in full Vietnamese dress, singing. It made me sick to my stomach when I saw that. So when I was at home slaving away, feeling trapped, taken for granted, power-less, ugly and full of hate for my life and existence, Mom was out having a wonderful time, singing and enjoying herself? I had always loved to sing and thought I had a great voice and a good ear for tone and music. I had, what most people would say natural talent. I could sing most songs on tune and can mimic and sound a lot like the original singer. But the only time I would sing was when I was alone in the house, when my brothers were gone with their friends or outside, and when my parents were gone. I would turn up the stereo and belt out the songs as if I was free. I would also dance around, just letting it go because for maybe one hour, there was nobody telling me I was stupid, ugly, worthless, too thin or too fat. And there was nobody telling me to stop singing, like Dad did when I was five.

I took a guitar class when I was 15 when I lived with the Gomez family, the second foster home I lived in, and the guitar instructor told me I was a natural. Jackie, the foster mother, had found a guitar that I could borrow so I could take the guitar class but after the class was over, I had to give the guitar back. I took another guitar class after high school but once again, I had to borrow a guitar. After the class was over, I still couldn't afford to buy a guitar. I just never thought I could pursue music because growing up, my parents didn't allow me to do any extracurricular activities in school. When I asked them about learning to play an instrument, Dad would say sarcastically, "Who's going to pay for it." He would say the same thing when I mentioned college.

If I had the opportunity to sit in front of a piano, which didn't happen very often, I would be able to play simple songs by ear and without notes because I didn't know how to read musical notes. So I would wish every now and then to learn to play an instrument and dream of singing but gradually, those desires and dreams died, because I didn't think it was possible for me to do any of those things.

Actually, I believed that the other reason why Mom was angrier towards me after her surgery was because she still had so much resentment towards her first husband, my biological father. It was because I reminded her of him, because I looked like him. I didn't know that until she gave me a picture of him when I was around 20. As soon as I saw the picture, which was a black and white portrait of his face, it explained so much. I obviously took after my biological father, with his darker skin and his wider and rounded nose. Interestingly, he had tight wavy hair, which I rarely saw among Asians. My hair was stick straight growing up but then in my twenties, it started becoming wavy. It seemed I took after him in that area too.

Mom would tell me that my biological father was handsome and tall, even though she didn't use the word biological. This was before she had shown me the picture. I wondered what is considered tall in Vietnamese. I didn't think he was handsome at all when I saw the picture of him and at the same time, I didn't think I was very pretty either. On a few occasions people have said I looked like Mom when they saw us together. I would look at them and say, "Really?" I couldn't see what they saw. I knew that if they saw the picture of my biological father, they wouldn't say that at all and would say instead that I looked more like him.

Because of all the medications she was taking, Mom developed a "moon face", causing her to feel self-conscious and worry about her appearance. For someone who was very petite and slim all her life, it was devastating to her to gain all this weight. Also, since she knew she only had five years left to live, she became even more envious of me. I was the one that got to live in the U.S. and my life certainly wasn't as hard as hers was so she had to make sure that I suffered as much as she did. Even though I didn't know at the time that she had only five years left to live, I did figure out that her gaining weight and developing the "moon face" made her become more envious of me. *How sick is that?* I thought. How could a mother be envious of her own daughter? I swore I would never treat my daughter the way Mom treated me.

# 12 Running Away

One day, when the restaurant was closed, I was at home alone with Mom. I had no idea where everyone else was, which was typical. As usual, Mom began reprimanding me and yelling at me. She kept lecturing me and at the same time beating me. It was the usual negative programming she inflicted, about how I was a bad child and how good I had it compared to her. As she was beating me with a wooden kitchen utensil, I sat crouched on the floor in the entry way of our house, covering my head with my hands and tucking my head in my knees. I tried hard to fight the tears but the more I fought the more she kept hitting me and trying to break me down. At one point the wooden spoon she had been using to hit me broke. You would think that she would have stopped hitting me at that point but she didn't. She was still not satisfied. So she went into the kitchen and got a knife, then began hitting me with the knife on its flat side.

At that point, I had had enough. I couldn't take it anymore. She was so full of rage. The hatred and anger I felt from her was so intense. I was afraid she was going to kill me. I wanted to get up and fight back and I wanted to hit her but I knew that would be wrong. I visualized myself getting up, then pushing and hitting her back. Certainly, I was stronger than her by now and I could easily overcome her, but I held back. In church, I learned that children should honor their parents. Also, Mom had instilled in me that there was nothing I could do, and that because she was the mother, she could do whatever she wanted. Basically, I had no worth and I was a nobody.

When she was finally satisfied with her venting, she stopped and went back into her room. I didn't know what she was going to do next but I knew I couldn't stay in the house, so I fled to my friend Lori's house. Lori lived one street over from me with her mother and two younger sisters. I don't know what drove me to flee that day. I hadn't thought about running to Lori's house before but something just snapped inside. I just couldn't stand to be home alone and trapped with Mom anymore. I couldn't understand why Dad and my brothers were always gone and were able to go wherever they wanted but *I* always had to be at home, which gave Mom the opportunity to verbally, mentally, and physically abuse me.

When I got to Lori's house, I frantically knocked on the door. Thank goodness they were home. Lori asked me what happened and after explaining it to her, she went and got her mother. I then told her mother what happened and that I just couldn't take it anymore. I knew Mom would come for me and sure enough, there was a pounding on the door. I was so afraid that I ran into one of the bedroom closets and crouched down in a fetal position and began to shake. I kept saying, "I don't want to go home. I don't want to go home." Then I heard the door open.

"Is Eden here?!"

"I'm sorry but you need to leave," Lori's mother replied.

"She here. I know it. You tell her come home now!"

"Eden is not going home. You need to leave or I will call the police on you. And don't you ever come back again!"

After I heard the door shut, I stayed in the closet until Lori told me that Mom was gone. I was so relieved. Lori knew how abusive Mom was. Lori's mother called someone from the Child Protective Service (CPS). I wondered how she knew to call them but I was glad she did. Somebody had to know what Mom was doing. I didn't know what was going to happen next. I knew that I might eventually have to go back home but thought I would let Mom simmer down for a while. How long that would take, I didn't know. I really hadn't thought anything through. I didn't know there was anything called CPS or that there was a foster home system. I just knew that something snapped inside and I just had to run. I also didn't know if Lori and her mother and sisters would be home or not, but I just had to take that chance. They were the only house I could think of going to and I was so thankful that they were home.

When the social worker arrived, he asked me some questions and examined my wounds from Mom beating me. Then he took me to the hospital for a more thorough examination. I was so relieved and thankful that I was under the care of another adult. I felt nervous but safe. As I sat on the examination table waiting for the doctor, the social worker and I calmly talked. Then the doctor came to take a look at me. They also took pictures of my arms, back, face, hands and legs. There was no blood or anything serious. Just a few bruises and a lot of red and raised welts, which had diminished in swelling by that time. After the examination, the doctor released me. The social worker filled out some paper work then took me to a receiving home. I was so glad I didn't have to go back home. We didn't even go back home to get any of my clothes.

The social worker took me to a house out in the country. It was a small white house with blue trim and steps going up to the front door. Inside, the floors were wooden. I had never been in a house with wood flooring before. The receiving home was run by a tall, big boned and slightly heavy set African American woman, who was possibly in her 50's. Ms. Jackson was a quiet lady and didn't talk much, but I did learn a few things from her. When she did talk, she talked slowly, with a low and calm voice. She also moved slowly and shuffled as she walked.

She was never in a rush and didn't seem too concerned about anything.

The receiving home was supposed to be a safe haven for children while they were awaiting for a decision to be made as to whether they should be returned to their family or be placed in a foster home. I didn't know what was going to happen to me but by that time, I realized I didn't want to go back home. I had gotten just a little taste of being away from home and some relief from my tyrannical mother and almost just as tyrannical and bullish older brother that it felt liberating. Strangely, I didn't worry about who would be working at the restaurant. I guessed that Tangela would be working at the restaurant more since I wasn't there.

At times, Ms. Jackson would have a baby to take care of, along with two or three other foster children. One of the rooms had a crib in it. The babies or children that came to the house could be there for one night or up to a couple of months. I was there for about one month before I had to go back home. Within a few days after my arrival, my parents came by to drop off some of my clothes. I remember seeing the family car parked on the street in front of the house, and them walking up to the house on the concrete walkway with Dad carrying a medium sized suitcase. It was just Mom and Dad. I opened the door and they handed me the suitcase. We didn't say very much to each other except that Mom said that I had put shame on her and the family. I guess I didn't think about what the neighbors would say or what her friends would think. I'm sure this would prove her case to her friends that I was a terrible and disobedient daughter. I didn't say anything back. There was nothing I could say to her that would change anything. There was no reasoning with her or trying to get her to understand where I came from. If she couldn't understand why she had so much anger and hatred towards me and why she was so intent on making my life miserable, there was no way she was going to understand why she needed to change or why she needed to stop beating me. And there was no way she would understand why I ran away. I guess she just expected me to keep accepting the abuse. That's what an obedient daughter would have done. Just keep taking the abuse and not talk back. I was being disobedient because I couldn't take the abuse anymore. I thanked them for bringing my clothes then they turned around and walked back to the car.

That one month living in the receiving home was filled with a lot of eye opening experiences. The children and other teenagers that came to stay at the receiving home were much more advanced than me in many ways. I had come from a very sheltered and restricted upbringing where I was not allowed to be out with friends or leave the house. Whereas most of these kids were not only older than me but they were used to being with other teenagers and out in the street. Some of them smoked and had boyfriends that they would have come over to the house when Ms. Jackson wasn't at home. And sometimes they would take off with their boyfriends. I didn't think they were allowed to leave but I knew there wasn't much I could do about it. I was 13 but I may as well have been 9 when it came to experiencing friendships and socializing.

One time, when Ms. Jackson was away working, one of the girls who was about 15 or 16 convinced me to go with her and one of her friends. I don't know if she was part of a gang or not but she had one of her "friends" pick her up. She mentioned something about going cruising. I didn't know what that meant. Next thing I know, I'm riding in the back seat of a low rider car being driven by a cholo wearing a blue bandana around his head. She told me we were going to a certain area of town that

I had never been to before. Well, it turns out that it wasn't the best part of town. We stopped at a few homes and she'd get out to talk to her friends. I would just stay in the car with her boy friend as he sat in the driver's seat. It felt surreal, like I was in a dream. I felt uneasy because I didn't know where we were, but I knew we were far away from the receiving home. I also didn't know who her friends were or her boy friend who was driving us around, and I really didn't know *her* for that matter. I wasn't much into cars but if I were, a low rider wouldn't have been my first choice.

Finally, after what seemed like a long day, we made it back to the receiving home. I swore I would never take off like that again with any of the other kids living there. I realized that I had put myself in a very precarious situation. Especially since there were no cell phones in case something happened. I also realized that somebody must have been watching over me because no harm was done to me. I was very thankful I made it back to the receiving home and nobody had tried to hurt me.

The kids that arrived would sometimes leave as fast as they came. They all seemed to like me since I never caused any problems or drama. When it was just Ms. Jackson and me, I would sit and watch her cook. I would offer to help her cook but she would always insist that she had it taken care of. It felt strange to have someone else cook for me without me helping out. One time, she had stepped away for a while to answer the phone. When she came back, the rice that had been cooking in a pot on the stove got a little burned. I had never seen rice being cooked on a stove like that before. I was used to seeing rice being cooked in a rice cooker. I asked her if she was going to throw the rice away. She said, "No, it'll be fine." Then she took a piece of white bread and laid it on top of the rice in the pot and put the lid back on. I asked her why she had done that.

She told me that the rice would absorb the burnt smell from the rice. After a few minutes, she removed the piece of bread and let me smell it. Sure enough, the bread smelled burned. I was so fascinated by that remedy and remembered it ever since.

The time came when the California Department of Social Services (DSS) made a decision on my case. Although there was a chance that I could be placed in a foster home, it was always best for the children to be reunified with their families to try and work things out. I was disappointed that I had to go back home but obviously had no choice. The DSS continued to provide services by assigning me a social worker that would meet with me and Mom approximately once a month to check on our progress. They also provided other services by means of family counseling. Mom and I had to go to weekly counseling for a while, which I thought would be a waste of time because I knew it wouldn't change anything. I knew Mom wouldn't change and I told the therapist so when I had an opportunity to talk to him alone.

"Just because we're going to counseling doesn't mean my mother's going to change. This isn't going to work. She's not going to change," I explained. I was certain of it.

"You know what? I believe you," he said. "You're probably right. Perhaps she won't change. But isn't it worth a try? Let's give it a try and see what happens."

The difficult part of the counseling was that I had to be in the room with Mom. With her in the room, I didn't feel I could speak freely. I was afraid that if I expressed my true feelings and thoughts that I would receive retaliation and get punished when I got home. I was able to convey though that I felt taken for granted, to which Mom had very little to say. I don't know if she really knew how to express appreciation. If she did, it was only to her friends.

It turned out that we only went to counseling a few times. Our assignment after our first session was that from now on, we had to say "thank you" and "please" to one another when talking to each other. This seemed to work for a while. When we returned for another session the therapist asked how things were going. Things were tense but seemed to be improving so we didn't need to resume counseling.

One of the rules my parents had to abide by was that they couldn't take me out of school to have me work at the restaurant like they had before. I also wasn't allowed to serve alcohol anymore so when someone ordered alcohol, Tangela, the cook, or Mom would have to serve it, if she was there. Things were fine for a few months. A social worker would come to the restaurant and meet with me and Mom. In one meeting, the social worker came to the restaurant in the afternoon, after the lunch rush had subsided and there was nobody else there.

As I sat facing Mom at one of the tables with the social worker sitting between us, I relayed to her my memory of the puppet I had made in the third grade and how Mom was very insensitive and critical, telling me to throw it away. Instead of complimenting me or ever telling me something positive, she was always putting me down and criticizing me. When I relayed the experience of how Mom told me to throw the puppet away, I got choked up and almost cried because the pain was still there. I guess I just didn't know how to recover from something like that. Then, to my surprise, Mom said that she didn't remember that incident and didn't remember saying or doing those things. I was devastated. That puppet meant so much to me because I had worked so hard on it, trying to be as unique and creative as I could. It was also the first art project I had ever brought home and yet she doesn't remember how cruel she was?

"You don't remember that?" I asked incredulously.

"No. I don't remember about that," Mom replied, seemingly surprised that I would remember something that occurred so long ago. The social worker intervened calmly and reminded Mom how important it is to be careful about the things that are said and about our actions because of how it could affect someone else.

For a little while, things seemed to be okay. But after a while, the monster began to rear its ugly head again. Mom began to slip back into her old ways. She started to unleash her anger on me again and hitting me again for no reason. One day, I came home from school and my clothes were strewn out on the front lawn. I felt so angry and humiliated as I picked up my clothes. I guess that was her way of saying that this was what I get for running away and not wanting to live at home. I just couldn't understand how a mother could treat her only daughter that way.

Then they had me work at the restaurant a couple of times instead of letting me go to school when there was a huge banquet that was taking place. Boy, were they going to get in trouble. This time, I had someone I could tell. Now I had someone I could talk to. Even though they didn't tell me not to say anything to the social worker, I knew that I was still going to even if they did.

Because Mom was reverting back to her old ways, I began to feel bad about myself again. I knew the counseling wasn't going to work! I sank back into feeling depressed even though I didn't know what depression was or had never heard of the word. Yet, I did know about feeling sad and miserable. So much so that I wanted to die. I didn't think my life was worth living. Not with Mom treating me the way she did. I wondered what I did to deserve this life and why did it have to happen to me, especially since I had it worse than my brothers. I also wished I had never been born. Because of the constant badgering and outbursts of unprovoked anger from Mom, I was a nervous wreck.

One day, when there were no customers in the restaurant, I was washing some of the drinking glasses in the part of the restaurant where all the drinking glasses, mugs, and wine glasses were stored. As I was washing one of the drinking glasses, it slipped out of my hands and fell onto the small metal sink. The drinking glass was slippery from the soap and from the yellow rubber gloves I was wearing that were too big for me, which made it difficult for me to get a firm grip on it. I had never broken anything in the restaurant before.

When Mom saw that I had broken one of the drinking glasses, she became angry at me. That was all she needed. "Do you know how much glass cost?!" she yelled. She began hitting me with her hands, but that was hurting her hands so she went into the office and found a wire hanger. She then took the hanger and began hitting me with it. I eventually sunk down to the floor and once again, curled into a ball, putting my head down and wrapping my arms around my legs so she couldn't hit my face. The blows kept coming down on my back, my arms, and my head, while at the same time, she's continuing to yell at me. Then suddenly, I felt something warm rolling down my face and the back of my head. I put my hands behind my head to find what it was. I felt a warm liquid and when I brought my hands in front of my face, I saw bright red blood on them. I was in disbelief and shock. When Mom saw that there was blood on my hands she finally stopped hitting me. Somehow, seeing the blood made her come to her senses.

She then helped me up and took me to the bathroom and helped me wash the blood off my hands and head. I didn't say anything to her because I was still in shock, and because there was nothing I could say. I just couldn't understand why she would become so violent about something that happened accidentally. I didn't do it on purpose. The glass was slippery from the soap and from the rubber gloves I was wearing that were too big. How could she think I did it on purpose?

While my head was lowered down close to the sink and the running faucet, Mom poured water over my head with her hands to wash off the blood. Suddenly, I heard her say in a low tone, "I sorry. I so sorry." I didn't say anything back to her. I was surprised to hear her say those words. I didn't expect her to ever say those words to me. I began to wonder how she would really feel if she actually did kill me. If she did kill me, who would help run the restaurant? It didn't make sense to me that she would treat me that way when she relied so much on me. Afterwards, I stayed in the bathroom, sitting on the hard tiled floor, and wishing I were dead. If I killed myself, would they finally feel bad that I wasn't around? Would I matter then? As usual, Dad and my brothers weren't around when this happened. Although I was glad to hear those words, I knew I couldn't let her get away with it. I knew I had to let my social worker know what happened, and I did.

That was the last straw. Because Mom had beaten me again and kept me away from school to work at the restaurant, my parents lost their rights to keep me. So I was taken from home and placed in a foster home.

# 13 The Grass Isn't Always Greener on the Other Side

The Grays had ten children, nine were girls and their youngest child was their only son. Five of the girls were grown and out of the home, some were married with kids of their own. They were a Portuguese family and the mother and father were first cousins. I was told that several of the girls had eye defects at birth, but they had corrective surgery so their eyes looked normal and you couldn't tell the ones that had previously been defective from the ones that were born with normal looking eyes.

However, Cheri's surgery didn't take and so her eyes remained defective. Her eyelids reminded me of when I saw kids rolling their top eyelids inside out. It seemed that Cheri tried to compensate for her looks by displaying a tough exterior. She was sort of the second in command next to Dorothy the mother, when it came to organizing the household of four other children that were still living at home besides herself, and the five foster children, myself included. She would walk around the house directing us to do this or that with her raspy voice.

Dorothy was a petite lady with big beautiful blue eyes and short curly, gray hair. You could tell she must have been very beautiful in her younger years and she was proud of showing you pictures of herself when she was younger. It's almost as if she expected you to compliment and praise her on the picture and comment how beautiful she was. These days, she was pudgier, but back in the day - well I guess that's what happens after having ten children. She was also quite the talker and a loud one at that. She had to be to get things done around the house. She would hurriedly walk around the house, directing someone to do this and that as she gestured with her arms and hands and pointed here and there.

Her husband, Bill, on the other hand, didn't talk much at all. When he got home from work, he didn't have to wait in line and was fed right away. After he was finished eating, he'd go to the family room, sit himself in a lazy chair and watch TV, while his only son would sit on the floor by his feet, looking up to him for any sign of attention. But Bill didn't talk to anyone, let alone the foster kids. I couldn't help but think how strange it was that he didn't to talk to anyone. What kind of father and role model was that? This was certainly not what I expected from a foster family. I quickly learned that the grass isn't always greener on the other side of the fence.

It was a little daunting at first, being surrounded by all these children and being the only Asian child in the home. However, I was so glad to be away from my family, especially from Mom, and away from the mental, emotional, and physical abuse. Finally, I thought, I would feel loved and receive the affection and attention I so desperately craved. I quickly learned though that just because a family or a couple have decided to open up their homes to take in children, coming from abusive and dysfunctional situations, it wasn't because they truly loved children. Surely the Grays had to love children to some extent because they had ten of their own. How could they not love children? Later, I learned that there were couples that truly did love children and wanted to help them; however, my experience with the Grays didn't lead me to know that. I soon learned instead that fostering children was just another source of income for them.

Since there were ten of us, and mostly girls, Mrs. Gray ran her home like a military boot camp. Although we had our own beds, we slept in two to four per room; we took showers in pairs, and waited our turn being fed, usually three at a time since the kitchen wasn't very big. We never ate at a dining table. There was a counter in the kitchen where there were three wooden chairs and that's where we would sit to eat, three at a time. We stood in line until someone had finished eating, then it was our turn at the counter. We were also given only one serving and I would often still feel hungry after eating. But I didn't dare ask for seconds. Every Friday night, we would have waffles for dinner. I had never had waffles before, let alone for dinner. It was different and I didn't mind it at first but having waffles every Friday for the one year I lived there grew a little old. Still, I accepted that routine since there wasn't much I could do about it, and I kept reminding myself that this was better than living at home.

When it came to bathing, us girls had to shower two at a time. The square shaped tiled shower stall was larger than most so that two people could fit in it. There was no tub and it was tiled on the floor as well as the three walls. After we finished our shower each night, we had to wipe down and dry the shower walls with a squeegee and towel. It was a routine that was programmed into me and to this day, I keep a squeegee in my bathroom and wipe down the shower stall before getting out. No matter where I lived, whether it was in a rented apartment or in my own home that I bought, I would go through this regimen of wiping down the shower stall with a squeegee, and then using the wrung out wash cloth to wipe the chrome fixtures dry, and any beads of water left on the shower walls. The only time I wouldn't wipe down the shower walls is when I am in a hotel or staying at a friend's home.

On the weekends, especially every Saturday, we were all assigned chores around the house. My job, along with two other foster kids, was to hand dust the entire collection of salt and pepper shakers that were displayed and stored in the long room that connected the two wings or sides of the house. On one side of the wing were the kitchen and the master bedroom. Nobody, at least none of the foster children, was ever allowed to see the master bedroom or any other rooms on that side of the house besides the kitchen. The other wing had the living room and family room where there was a pool table, and the other bedrooms where the children and foster children slept.

Dorothy had the largest collection of salt and pepper shakers I had ever seen. She could actually open up a shop of just salt and pepper shakers. Most of them were ceramic but there were others made from non-ceramic materials, such as wood, metal, and glass. Her collection was so vast and prolific, and the themes ranged from animals, plants, and food, to people, kids and buildings. They came in all different sizes and colors and there were no two pairs alike. It took three children in that long hallway-like room to dust each and every salt and pepper shaker every Saturday.

When I realized that my dream of having a loving and affectionate family was not going to materialize living with the Grays, I became despondent. There was no privacy and I was just another mouth to feed. Just like living at home, who I was or what kind of special talents or gifts I might possess was never investigated or inquired about. I was just a means to bring extra income to the Grays. Because there wasn't anyone I could talk to at the home, I began to write my frustrations and feelings in a journal. When I received calls from my social worker, I would tell them that things were okay. But I would also express my concerns of not having enough to eat and that living with the Grays was not exactly what I'd expected. Still, it was better than where I was because at least, I wasn't being physically, emotionally, and mentally abused by my mother. Little did I know, however, that Dorothy was listening to my phone calls.

One evening, as I was sitting on my bed reading, Vicky, one of Dorothy's daughters came into my room and asked how I felt about living with her family. I did my best to point out the positives of living with her family; however, the more she probed the more I learned that her mother had been eavesdropping on my phone conversations with my social worker and friends from church. I was devastated and felt so violated. Then Dorothy came into the room and informed me that she had read my diary and was concerned about the things I had written. How dare she read my personal feelings! I had no one to talk to about my feelings and experiences and the only thing I had was to write them in my diary. How could she do such a thing?!

However, instead of telling her my true feelings about how angry, hurt, and violated I felt, I apologized for not being the happy foster child she wanted me to be. I knew though that she really wasn't interested in my happiness. It was just all for show so that she could collect the $500 per child each month. No, a foster child could not tell their social worker how things really were like, living at the Grays because Mrs. Gray would hear what you said. At least on the phone I couldn't. Fearing retribution, I decided to tell her what she wanted to hear.

But when I would have my visits with my social worker, I did tell her how things were. Like how I still felt hungry after eating and was afraid to ask for seconds. It was just something I felt and knew not to do. Possibly because I never saw any of the other foster kids ask for seconds.

We also weren't allowed to make a telephone call when we wanted to. We had to ask for permission but most of the time, I was too afraid and intimidated to ask. Besides, why bother because Dorothy would listen in on the phone conversation anyway. The only time I would talk on the phone then, is if someone was to call me. Therefore, I couldn't talk to my best friend Lori every day like I used to. At least I would see her at school. I would also talk to Dad if he called, which wasn't very often. One day, when Dad called, I learned that my parents ended up selling the restaurant after about a year since I had been gone. When I heard that, I felt glad and had a sort of "I told you so" attitude. Clearly, my parents couldn't run the restaurant without me. Then hiring someone else full-time to wait on tables was just too expensive and would cut into their profits. Plus, the waitress probably would have taken more of the tips when I wasn't allowed to take any. Besides, I don't know if Mom worked at the restaurant more after I left but I couldn't imagine her waiting on tables. She already had a cook and if she had cooked more, that could have helped to improve business since I thought her cooking was a lot better than the hired cook. That way, people would want to come back more often because of the good food. But my parents didn't think the way I did. Oh well, that was no longer my problem. I felt that my parents, especially Mom, deserved to lose the restaurant.

This made me think of the money that my parents had put away for my brothers and me before they bought the restaurant. They had opened a savings account for each of us kids and we got five dollars a month as an allowance. My brothers and I heard about other kids getting allowances and when we asked our parents about it, they refused to give us one. However, they decided to open the savings accounts for us, except we couldn't touch it. We also had a piggy bank that was supposed to be for us kids too but twice, my parents broke into it because they needed the money. When I watched Mom break the ceramic piggy bank the second time, I was sad. I knew that the family needed money but that was *our* money. It seemed that whenever we needed something, there just wasn't enough and saving up for it wasn't working either. I felt like Mom was constantly lying to us.

Anyway, after I was placed into the foster care system, my parents kept the money that was in "my savings" account. I never saw any of it even though I felt I had worked every day of my life. When I asked about it, Dad told me that they had to use the savings account to pay for me being in a foster home. I didn't realize that my parents had to pay a certain amount to the county every month for me living in a foster home.

While I was living with the Grays, I began studying the Bible on a weekly basis with one of the women that went to the church Lori went to. Brenda lived nearby so she would pick me up and take me to her home and we would study for about an hour and then she would take me back to the Grays. I enjoyed the Bible studies as it was a way for me to learn new things and to get answers to the questions I had about life, like why we are here, and what the future holds. It was also a way for me to have a break from being at the Grays.

For some reason, when I was younger, around seven or eight, I had this fear of the world being destroyed and the earth was going to split in two. I had images of the earth cracking open and people trying to avoid the deep crevices that were widening because the world was falling apart. I had no idea where these fears and images came from. Perhaps it was just hearing about the war going on in the news or hearing Dad talk about when he was in Vietnam, but I couldn't be sure. I don't recall watching much TV or watching the news if I did. So these images and fears made me want to know what the future held for humans and for the planet. Thankfully, I got my answers through the Bible studies.

I guess I had always been spiritual-minded and at the time, it was reflected in my interest in the Bible. When my brothers would be outside playing with their friends, I would be inside the house, reading the comic version of the Bible, which was a thick and big book that had colored pictures and dialogues of the Bible stories. I don't know how or when it came into our home but I'm pretty certain that it was through Mom. The comic pictures made it a lot easier to read and understand the Bible stories. Other than that, the only other Bible we had was one that Mom had in Vietnamese, which I couldn't read.

Even though I was curious to learn what the Bible said, it never occurred to me that when I went to Mass, the priest rarely read out of the scriptures or had us open the Bible to read from it. Not until I went to the same church that Lori went to did I notice that. So unlike Mom telling me stories without any reference to the Bible and which didn't make any sense to me, through the weekly Bible studies with Brenda, I received answers straight from the Scriptures, which did make more sense to me. Brenda would also pick me up every Sunday to go to church, where I would see Lori and meet other people.

As I continued to go to church on a regular basis and meet other people there, I came to learn what loving people did. The people were kind, friendly, and warm, and seemed very genuine. They were always happy to see me and they also seemed to care about me. I could also tell there was love among the families.

# 14 It's Not the Destination

One of the loving couples I met at the church was Jackie and Jacob Gomez. Jackie was originally from England and Jacob was Mexican but from the U.S. They had met when Jacob was in the Army and stationed in Britain. They came to the U.S. where they got married and had six children. They had three boys and three girls. When I met them, five of their children were already grown up and out of the house. Their oldest child and daughter was a single parent with two girls who were one and two years younger than me. Their second daughter was married with kids, two of their sons were married and the third son, at the time, was going through a divorce. And all of their names began with the letter "J".

When I first met Jackie at my junior high school graduation through my friend Lori, she seemed like a very kind, generous, and loving person. She was also very knowledgeable and versed in the scriptures. I had a lot of questions and I was impressed with how she was able to explain things and give me the answers to my questions by using the scriptures instead of telling me stories or legends like Mom did. So I continued to keep myself open to learning more, despite Mom not wanting me to get involved with Lori's church.

Because I was attending church regularly, I got to know more people in the congregation and most everyone knew of my situation of living in the foster home. Not because I told everyone, but word gets around. It was like one big family. Jackie also knew of my family history and the foster home environment that I was living in so she and Jacob decided to get their license to become a foster parent. When Jackie told me what they were doing, I was thrilled and felt so honored. I couldn't believe they would go through the process of getting licensed to become a foster parent for me. It was difficult for me to understand how some people could be so giving and kind, especially towards me. Yet, they loved children and they loved helping others in the congregation.

When the Gomez's finally finished all their courses and training, I was able to move in with them, which was in town. By that time, it had been about one year that I lived with the Grays. *Finally*, a family who actually liked me and were able to show me love. Plus, I would have a younger "sister" that I could have a relationship with. The plan was for me to now have my weekly Bible studies with Jackie from that point on because I had formed a good relationship with her and it was more convenient for me to study with her instead of Brenda, who lived out in the country.

Things were very different living with the Gomez's than with the Gray's. I had my own room and things seemed peaceful and stable, at least initially. I wasn't used to that but was thankful and appreciative for what they had done. They really had a different outlook on life and how children were to be treated. Once, when I accidentally tipped over a glass of milk that I was drinking with a snack and broke the glass, I was surprised at the difference in the reaction to what happened. After I had cleaned up the spill and put the pieces of broken glass in the trash, I went to Jacob, who was in his bedroom taking a nap. Jackie wasn't home so I went to Jacob to tell him what had happened. He sat up in his bed and asked me if I was okay. *Of course I was okay*, I thought. Wow, he was actually concerned about my safety?

"But what about the glass? Will Jackie get upset that I broke it?"

"No, don't worry about that. What matters is that you didn't get hurt," he replied.

Wow, what a huge difference. I didn't tell him about what happened when I accidentally broke a glass at my parents' restaurant. There was no need. It was different here and that was all that mattered. The other thing I had to get used to was Jackie doing most if not all of the cooking. I would offer to help because that was what I was used to doing. But Jackie cooked vastly different things than what I learned to cook. She made a lot of very healthy dishes, homemade bread, homemade yogurt, and other things I never heard or knew of. Not that I didn't prepare healthy meals, it was just more Vietnamese dishes that Mom showed me, mostly stir fry. Jackie would have this saying about bread. "The whiter the bread, the sooner you're dead." This was because she would make whole grain breads instead of having us eat white bread bought in the store. I learned quite a bit from Jackie and enjoyed the foods that she would make. Jackie and Jacob really did their best to make me feel at home and part of the family.

When it came to school pictures, they even put my portrait up with the other family photos in their living room. It felt strange for me to see my picture next to their youngest daughter Jessica's and other family photos. I wasn't fond of seeing pictures of myself and wasn't used to seeing them in a frame and on display in the home. Most of my own family pictures were in albums that were stored away. I felt a little embarrassed that my picture was with theirs.

The Gomez's would also frequently have visitors over, mostly it would be their oldest daughter Jamie who lived in town and who had two daughters. Jamie was divorced so she was raising the two girls on her own. Because Jamie was quite a bit older than Jessica, her two daughters who were Jessica's nieces were actually older than Jessica. The Gomez's would also have the guest speaker from the Sunday services over for lunch, and other friends from the congregation. The house always seemed to be buzzing with people coming and going and Jackie's schedule was busy as well. She cleaned homes to bring in additional income for the family since Jacob was already retired. She not only made a lot of healthy homemade foods but she also sewed. Jackie was so busy that we would rarely have time for my weekly Bible studies, which was something I really wanted to have. I enjoyed learning about how to be a happier person, about family life, what God expected of me, and what the future holds for the planet and the people living on it. That way too, I could have some one on one time with Jackie. But Jackie had a difficult time finding time to do that. She didn't even have time to study with her own daughter Jessica.

Jackie had Jessica at age 41, which back then, was a big deal. Jackie was very proud of the fact that she had another healthy child at that age because she lived such a healthy lifestyle. She ate healthy and made sure her family did as well. She exercised regularly and had lots of energy. She was also very active in the congregation.

Jessica was about four years younger than me and was as spoiled as can be. She wasn't the innocent little girl most people thought she was. She was practically an only child since her older siblings were out of the house by the time she was born. So whatever Jessica wanted, Jessica got. Things were fine in the beginning but over time, Jessica would start to accuse me or blame me for things she had done. For example, she would leave the curling iron on in the bathroom and when Jackie would discover that it had been left on, Jessica would immediately blame me without thinking twice. At first, I questioned whether I had done it or not but after a while it kept happening and I knew I hadn't left it on. When something is brought to my attention, I try not to repeat the mistake. I was sensitive that way. I received enough negative attention from Mom and the last thing I wanted was to get in trouble. So when it kept happening and Jessica would immediately blame me, I began to speak up and defend myself. I realized after a while that I had to stay on my toes because Jessica wouldn't take any responsibility for anything she did and lied just about everything.

Also, when Jackie or Jacob wasn't home, Jessica would start having boys come over to the house. She wouldn't have them come into the house itself because that would not have been allowed, especially since I would be in the house to see what she was doing, but she would sneak them into the back yard and hang out with them. It made me feel very uncomfortable when she did that because she was only 11 and these were boys from school and not from church. I had been learning to be careful of who I associated with so that I don't become influenced to do bad things, like smoking, getting into drugs, or getting into a relationship with a boy or dating when I was not ready for marriage. I kept hearing over and over, "Bad associations spoil useful habits." I was certain that Jessica knew these things also so I couldn't understand her behavior. I guess when I was told to do or not to do something, I always obeyed because for me, there were always consequences.

Then, when it came to Jessica's two nieces, Dawn and Debby, who were a few years older than her but younger than me, they too were starting to "get into boys". One day, Dawn, the older of the two nieces and who was 13 asked me if I liked boys. I couldn't believe she had asked me that! I was surprised to hear her question because I thought that she and Debbie should know better. Didn't they go to the same church that I was going to and didn't they hear the same message that I did? It wasn't so much that I wanted to be a goody two shoes. I was just trying to apply what I had been learning through church and through my Bible studies. I learned from going to church that if you learned a Bible principle but didn't apply it, it was as if you didn't know the Bible principle at all.

Besides, I couldn't even begin thinking about boys. All I could think about was survival and staying out of trouble. I wanted to know that there would be a better life for me than what I had before and that the earth would stay intact and not fall apart. I wanted to learn how to be happy and what I could do to live a happy life. I also believe that on a subconscious level I wanted to understand why Mom hated me so much. It was the one thing that still occupied a lot of my mind even though I thought that I had moved on and that my unhealthy relationship with her was behind me. It was sort of like a mystery or puzzle that I wanted to solve. When I was living at home, I couldn't have any friends, let alone a boyfriend. Somehow, I just knew I was too young to even go there. I also wanted to know if there were people that really loved me. I guess without really realizing it, I was looking for love and trying to understand what it was. However, I knew that getting involved with a boy at such a young age wasn't the answer. Perhaps it was my mother's example that made me realize that.

Dawn was only 13 and her sister Debbie was 12. It wasn't just their age that bothered me but it was also because they went to the same church as me. Where were their minds? I couldn't understand why they would be interested in boys, especially ones that didn't go to the same church as we did and who probably didn't have the same values as we did. At least that was what we were being taught. All I knew to do was what I was told. I didn't know how to rebel, how to be defiant or how to throw a tantrum. At home, I couldn't get away with anything. I couldn't even get away with just existing and no matter what I did, it wasn't good enough. So how I could I go against something that I was being taught is wrong to do? Also, the way they talked and the language that they used were not what I was learning to be very Christian. Then, I saw their mother doing things and it made me question a lot of things about the Gomez family. Perhaps that's why Dawn and Debbie felt it was okay to do the things they did because their mother either didn't care or didn't think there was anything wrong with what they were doing.

The one person I didn't feel I had to question was Jacob, who was a very kind, gentle, humble, and easy going man. I felt he was genuine and wasn't trying to hide anything or be something different than what he was. He rarely got upset or raised his voice unless Jessica did something to push him. Although I learned that he wasn't always that way. When Jackie first started studying the Bible and going to church, Jacob was violently opposed but over time, he was won over through her persistence and good example. He then joined her in attending church and becoming an active member of the congregation.

After a while, it seemed I was constantly on the edge of being pulled into doing things I knew I shouldn't by the girls, even though they were younger than me. So I would talk to Jackie about what I had been observing and began to ask her questions about proper Christian conduct even though I pretty much knew the answers. I was confused and conflicted as to what I saw and what I was learning. The girls had known this information long before I did so I couldn't understand why they weren't applying what they had been taught. I also would hear from our Sunday service talks about leading double lives. So I began telling Jackie the things I had been observing from

Jessica, Dawn, and Debbie. Well, that didn't sit too well with Jackie. For some reason, she didn't want to admit that her granddaughters and her youngest daughter would do anything wrong. She had a strong reputation at church and there was no way anyone was going to ruin it.

I soon saw that Jackie had a lot of pride in herself and her family. She had worked hard to help other people and she received a lot of recognition from the other church members. One time, when we were at an Assembly, where several congregations got together a couple times a year to share experiences, testimonials, stories, and to learn more about what it means to be a Christian, Jackie had a part in the program. She had shared her experience of when she first started attending church and studying the Bible and how her husband was very opposed. But then how he was won over by her good conduct and changed in personality for the better. He went from being an angry, domineering, and violent husband to being humble, kind and loving. It was a very encouraging story of courage and perseverance and I felt the recognition was well deserved. She was a hard worker and genuinely did want to help others.

While she was on stage, many of her family members and I were seated in the same row as her in the audience. Jackie had been sitting in the second seat next to an aisle and I was about several seats down from her. Then I got up to go to the restroom. Jackie was still backstage and hadn't returned to her seat yet. When I returned from the restroom to go to my seat, I saw that it had been taken by one of Jackie's granddaughters. Then, somebody else had occupied Jackie's seat so I sat down where I saw the nearest seat available was, which was closer to the aisle than where I was before. I don't know why things got shifted around but they did. Then when Jackie came back from backstage and returned to her seat, she saw that it was occupied so she scooted passed several people to get to an available seat. She had to step passed six or seven people before she finally reached an empty seat. After a few minutes she got up and went to the back of the assembly room.

When we were dismissed for a lunch break, I went to the back where there were tables for people to eat their lunch. I saw Jackie at one of the tables with tears in her eyes and she was holding her forehead with her hand. I asked her what was wrong. She told me that after giving her experience on stage, she thought she deserved a little more respect than to have to step through all those people to get to a seat. She told me that she felt humiliated and felt someone should have gotten up to let her sit down closer to the aisle. I was really surprised to know that's what she had been upset about. Those people again were her family members and even though she was so giving and generous to them, I could see that they had taken her for granted and didn't really appreciate all the things she did for them. I informed her that someone had taken my seat and if I had known how she felt, I would have given up my seat for her. I really didn't know how else to respond to her or console her. I had no idea that she would make such a big deal about the seating. She had seemed so humble on stage.

As time went on, it became more uncomfortable living with the Gomez's and things became tense and awkward. Jackie was constantly busy and didn't have time to study with me or her daughter Jessica. After living with the Gomez's for about a year, I could count the number of times I had my week-ly Bible study on one hand. Jackie soon saw the need to study with Jessica again as she noticed her behavior was getting worse. Jessica was beginning to act out and throw temper tantrums. So she made an attempt to start having weekly Bible studies with Jessica but that lasted only a few weeks and then they stopped again. She just didn't have the time or energy to do it. Finally, as I shared with my social worker what was occurring with the Gomez's, she decided to find another foster home for me. However, I informed my social worker that I wanted to continue attending church and I was granted that right to do so.

## Every Family Has Secrets

Raquel Soares was a tall lady in her fifties with blue eyes and light blond hair that she always kept swept up in a beehive. She had been divorced for many years and all her children were grown and out of the house. She had three daughters and one son. She also had a tiny little white dog named Mitzy whom most people would consider spoiled because she would sometimes get cooked steak or chicken that Raquel would cut up into little pieces. Occasionally, Raquel would buy Kentucky Fried Chicken just for Mitzy. Besides Mitzy, Raquel also had two Doberman Pinchers who were intimidating to me at first but I later grew accustomed to them. They weren't allowed in the house like Mitzy was, so the only time I had to interact with them was when I wanted to sit outside under the covered patio of the back yard.

I didn't know if Raquel ever had any other foster children prior to me but I was the only one that lived with her while I was there. Raquel was a bus driver and a caterer. During the summer months when she didn't have to drive the buses, she would do more catering jobs. Raquel's house was very clean and similar to when I lived at the Gray's, I had chores to do. Every Saturday, I had to dust the house and clean the bathroom that I used. Also, in the living room, which was rarely ever used, there was one wall that was all mirrors, from the ceiling down to the floor. I had to clean that wall of mirrors each week as part of my chores, whether they looked dirty or not. Although I didn't mind having the chores, I still couldn't help but feel like I was some type of free labor. Still, I was thankful to be there since it was much quieter and peaceful, at least when it was just the two of us.

Every now and then, one or two of her daughters would come and visit. Rarely would all three be at the house at the same time. Sometimes they would stay the night and other times, it would just be for a few hours. Whenever her daughters came over, I would ask a lot of questions. There was so much I wanted to learn about life, relationships, God, and many other things. Raquel's oldest daughter Madeline, who looked different than the two younger daughters because she had dark brown hair instead of red like Linda's and Rebecca's, once told me that she had burned up all her Beatle's albums after John Lennon said that the Beatles were more popular than Jesus Christ. She had a strong faith in Jesus and was offended by what he had said. I didn't know of the incident of course, and was surprised to learn that she would take such drastic and bold action upon hearing his claim.

Soon, I began to learn that just like any other family, there would be conflicts and arguments between Raquel and her children. For some reason, the middle daughter Linda was sort of treated like an outcast by the other two daughters. I didn't always know what they were arguing about but I got the sense that there were some old issues and wounds that hadn't been dealt with and something to do with Linda being the favorite daughter. I would sometimes hear someone talk about something that happened when they were younger or how Raquel had raised them. I never liked seeing people argue or to see conflict so I stayed out of the way as much as possible, especially since I felt it was none of my business. So I would just retreat to my room.

Her son Andrew stayed with us one time and it made me feel uneasy. Being a teenager and feeling vulnerable, it made me feel especially uncomfortable when it was just the two of us at home. Apparently, he was having some issues with his wife and so he came to live with Raquel for a while. He was friendly enough and tried to talk to me but there was always something there telling me to be cautious. He finally did move back to his family in the Los Angeles area.

Now that I was 15, I was able to start working so I obtained a worker's permit and got a part-time job working at the high school office during the summer months. Because I didn't have a driver's permit yet and didn't have a car, I would walk to work. It felt strange to be at the high school when there weren't any students around. It was very quiet on campus. I learned some new skills while on the job and my supervisor was very happy with my work and attitude. I could tell she liked me and always commended me for doing a great job, which was awkward to receive but nice to hear. I rarely heard or received compliments at home but graciously accepted it. I felt like I just did my job and minded my own business. I asked a lot of questions and always seemed to keep myself busy without having to be told what to do all the time. And once I learned something, I got it and didn't need to be told again and again how to do it. I guess I was used to that since I had so much to do at home and knew that if I didn't, I would get in trouble. My supervisor was so pleased with my work that she wrote a letter of recommendation for me when that summer assignment was over.

After I finished working at the high school, I got a job as a waitress working at a restaurant chain called Happy Steak. I figured that my previous experience working at my parents' restaurant would come in handy, even though I was still very shy. However, I wanted to start earning money so I could buy new clothes and other things that a teenage girl would need. I found that living in a foster home didn't necessarily mean all your needs would be provided for you. Basically, you received a place to live and food to eat. If you needed dental, vision, or medical care, the County would pay for those needs. And even though the foster parents were given a clothing allowance, the only foster parent that ever bought me clothes was Jackie. At the same time, I would also sew my own clothes when I lived with the Gomez's and with Raquel.

I also wanted to grow up fast so I could be on my own and not have to deal with living with people who really didn't love me or care for me. I just couldn't wait to become an adult.

Working at Happy Steak was very different than working at my parents' restaurant. There were other waiters and waitresses that worked there. There were busboys, several cooks, and a manager, who was originally from Fiji, that ran the restaurant and who cooked as well. I was very nervous when I first started. It had been a while since I waited on tables and dealt with the public in that way. I was nervous also because of how Rick, the manager who hired me dealt with me. He would often talk to me in an abrupt and condescending tone, as if he was irritated. I found out that I wasn't the only one he addressed in that manner.

This made me feel intimidated by him so I told him that one day. Rick was cooking and I was the only waitress working that shift. In our conversation and for some reason I don't recall, I admitted to him, "Well, I feel intimidated by you."

Rick chuckled sarcastically and said, "Is that right? Why is that?"

"I don't know. You just make me feel intimidated," I replied boldly.

I have no idea why or how I was able to be so bold and straight forward towards him. I had never said that to anyone, sharing how I felt or what I was thinking. It wasn't as if he made me feel comfortable to say that either. Perhaps I thought that if I told him that, he would stop talking to me the way he did. But it didn't work.

Rick told me when he first hired me that he just needed me part-time and that as time went on, depending on how I do, he could give me more hours, which was fine with me. However, he would not place me on the schedule that he made at least a week in advance. Everyone else that worked there, including himself was on the schedule except for me. Perhaps he felt I wasn't confident enough. One time he asked me, "You said you worked at a restaurant before?" I confirmed that I did. However, I didn't go into the detail of saying that it was at my parents' restaurant when I was 12. I didn't want him to really know how long ago it was and that I may not have been as competent and experienced as he thought I was.

Perhaps he picked up on my awkwardness and insecurity after all and that's why he wouldn't put me on the schedule. Instead, he would call me to let me know when he needed me. That was fine for a while but after several weeks, I asked him to please put me on the schedule like everyone else. He told me that he would, however, a few weeks went by and he still had not put me on the schedule and continued to call me in to work whenever he wanted. I asked him again to put me on a work schedule. Finally he did. Except when I would look at the times I was scheduled to work, he would tell me I didn't have to work. Then, when it was supposed to be my day off, he'd call me in. I got confused and frustrated with what he was doing.

Finally, one day when I was scheduled to be off, I had made plans to do things with a friend from church who had a car. Lana, who was African American and around 21, had a VW Beetle and we were going to go shopping. Sure enough, Rick called me in to come to work. I told him that he had me down on the schedule as having the day off and that I already had plans for the day so I wouldn't be able to come in. This made Rick angry. So he irately said, "I don't need you then! Don't bother coming in again!" I thought that was just fine because I didn't think it was fair the way he dealt with me.

A week later, I came in to pick up my last paycheck. It was during a week day and before the dinner rush. When I walked into the restaurant, I noticed that all the lights were off. There were no customers at any of the tables and when I got to the back of the restaurant where the kitchen was, I noticed that all of my former coworkers were just hanging out. All the cooks, waitresses, and waiters were sitting around and talking. I asked them what they were all doing here. They told me that they had all quit. I didn't believe them. "Really? You guys are kidding right?" I asked.

"No. We quit. We heard what Rick did to you so we decided to quit. We're tired of his bullshit and how he treats us. And we didn't think it was right what he did to you so we're all quitting."

I was still in disbelief that they would all quit on account of what happened to me but here they all were. Nobody was working. They were just sitting around talking and waiting for Rick to come. I knew that Rick wasn't the most pleasant person to work for and I knew other coworkers were frustrated with him as well. Most of them had worked there longer than I had and I would hear of other employees who had quit in the past because of him, but I didn't realize that they had the same level of frustration that I did while working there.

"What are you guys going to do?" I asked.

"We can find other jobs."

I wished them well and went home, still not really believing that they had all quit at the same time on account of what happened to me. I thought that Rick would probably be able to get some of them to stay and work for him. He just had a way of doing and saying the right things when he wanted something. Unfortunately, I never really kept in contact with the other employees so I never knew for sure what happened later.

After I told Raquel what happened, she told me that I could work for her, instead of me looking for another job. I could help her with her catering business and she would pay me a little more than minimum wage. So I agreed. It was actually fun working for Raquel. While she made the main dishes, I would create these large and elaborate vegetable trays. She would just let me do what I wanted so I would create some pretty amazing trays. I would make bridges out of the baby carrots and all kinds of neat designs. The ones she made herself before I helped her were pretty simple. Soon, she began to get compliments on the vegetable trays so that made her trust me even more. Although I would help with some of the other dishes, my main job was putting the vegetable trays together. I had a lot of fun creating the different designs and never made the same design twice.

Soon, Raquel's catering business was really taking off so she decided to turn her garage into a kitchen. After a while, she had me come with her to the parties whereas before, I would just work at home. It was a lot of hard work, carrying large dishes and containers of food, but at least I felt that I got paid well for it since it was more than what I had been paid at my other jobs.

At one wedding reception, I wore a pink dress that I had sewn. She had one hired helper who couldn't come to help her that day so she had me come instead. One of the groom's men noticed me and commented on how hard he saw me work. He complimented my dress and how he noticed I was carrying these heavy steel rectangular chafing dishes that were full of food. Even though I accepted the compliment, it made me feel nervous so I diverted the attention to Raquel, directing my arm towards her and saying how she was the main person responsible. He acknowledged that she did a great job but he also wanted to recognize me as well. In that brief interaction, I began to have the feeling that he had a little crush on me, which made me feel even more nervous. So I thanked him again and didn't say anything else. I didn't know what else to say to him. Later, after the reception was over, I thought about how stupid I was for diverting the compliment back to Raquel and not graciously accepting it. Of course she did a great job. She was the main person who put this all together. I realized he was trying to focus in on me.

I didn't know it at the time but later I learned that when someone compliments me, I should just be thankful and not say anything else. I also learned that if I received a gift, I should just be thankful and gracious as well for the gift. It took me a long time to really understand that concept and to believe that I deserved to receive praises and gifts. I realized later that one of the reasons why it was so difficult for me to be a gracious receiver was because I rarely ever received compliments from my parents when I was at home, and I rarely ever saw them be gracious receivers. Whenever I wanted to get something for Dad for his birthday, he would always reply firmly, "Ahhh, I don't need anything. Don't worry about it." This would make me feel sad and disappointed, and the joy and excitement of giving him something was quickly extinguished.

When it was Mom, she rarely said thank you and had an air of entitlement, even though we had to say please and thank you as children. She also demanded this or that from me so I couldn't give from a willing heart. Soon, I began to realize that how my parents responded in the way they received was how I felt as well. Not so much that I felt I was entitled but more so that I didn't deserve it.

Raquel really was a wonderful cook. One of my favorite dishes that she made was her chili beans. When I lived at home with my family, Dad would cook every now and then and one of the dishes that he cooked a lot for dinner was chili beans. Aside from cooking the traditional holiday meals where we would have turkey or ham, mashed potatoes and a salad, it seemed that was all he would cook because that was what he learned to cook in the military. After a while, I couldn't stand to eat chili beans anymore. He also would make pancakes for breakfast quite frequently. He would slice bananas and put them in the pancakes. When I told my school friends that Dad did that, they thought it sounded gross. They never had bananas with their pancakes and thought it was weird. Since I didn't cook breakfast, Dad would get up early and make the pancakes. I would ask him what was for breakfast and he'd always say, "Pancakes." It was the same thing almost every morning. After a while, I don't know why I even bothered asking. Because of having pancakes so often, when I got out on my own, I didn't eat pancakes for years.

Nevertheless, even though I was sick of eating chili beans because Dad made it so much, once I tasted Raquel's, my taste for it was renewed. I even told her about Dad's chili beans but that I really liked hers. She would usually just make it for her catering parties so we didn't have it all the time. Therefore, sometimes I would ask her to make it just for us because I liked it so much, and she would.

Things were pretty peaceful when it was just Raquel and me. However, I noticed that she too just wanted to keep me at home and not let me spend time away from home unless it was for school or work. I also came to believe that she was a bit prejudiced when it came to African Americans. That one time that I wanted to spend time with my friend Lana, Raquel wasn't too pleased with me hanging out with her. She made some comment about her being African American, which surprised me and made me realize that she didn't like Lana just because of her skin color. She didn't know Lana and even though Lana was someone from church, she still didn't trust her. After that time, she wouldn't allow me to do anything else with Lana.

As Raquel's daughters became more used to me being there, they also became more comfortable in showing their displeasure with Raquel. They would argue with her and it made me feel very uncomfortable. I just didn't feel like I was really a part of a family and wanted to keep myself away from their disagreements.

When Raquel and her daughters decided to go down to Southern California for a vacation and to visit her son, I didn't want to go. I wasn't comfortable being around her and all her adult children. I just wanted to stay at home and be by myself, go to church and be with my friends from church.

However, she wouldn't allow it. "I have to be responsible for you. In case something happens to you, I would be the one responsible." Even though logically what she said made sense, I really felt that she said those things just to manipulate or control me. But I didn't know what to say to convince her to let me stay at home while she went on her vacation. My parents left me and my brothers home alone when I was 11 and even though Luc was 13, he may as well have been 11 too due to his immaturity. She also said, "Most kids would be thrilled to go on a vacation like this and I am paying for you to go." She mentioned Universal Studios, Disneyland, Beverly Hills, and Hollywood. That still didn't convince me. I just didn't like being around her and her daughters because they seemed to argue a lot. And because her daughters were much older, I just didn't feel that I really fit in or that it felt like a family.

Obviously, I had no choice but to go. It was a long drive there and thankfully, I don't remember much of it. I do remember going to Universal Studios and being really scared when we went through the Jaws ride. I also remember Disneyland, how crowded it was so that you could barely walk and move around. I had never seen masses of people walking around like that before. Then waiting in the long lines for an hour or so for the rides wasn't fun either. However, once we got on, it was pretty fun. Still, I didn't feel comfortable overall. I just didn't feel like I fit in with the family and that I belonged there.

Andrew also drove us down Sunset Boulevard, which was a very eye opening experience for me. There were many billboards and signs soliciting nude women. It wasn't something I was used to seeing. We also drove around Beverly Hills and saw the beautiful homes that the celebrities lived in.

We stayed at Andrew's little house where he, his wife, and children lived. I and one of Raquel's daughters slept on the living room floor while another daughter slept on the couch. The house wasn't as clean as I was used to and that made me feel uncomfortable as well. The floor was dirty and there was mold in the shower stall and even after taking a shower, I still felt dirty. I had gotten used to Raquel's standard of cleanliness and was surprised that her son, one of her family members would live so differently from her.

One night, while trying to go to sleep, I could hear Raquel, her son and two of her daughters arguing. I don't remember or know what they were arguing about but as Raquel came into the living room where I laid on the floor trying to sleep, I heard her say, "Well, I guess I should just get a gun and shoot myself!" I was horrified and began to cry silently as I lay there on the floor. What was so important that they had to argue about it so late at night? And why was Raquel talking about killing herself? Then I heard something about Raquel drinking too much. With all that going on, how could I sleep? I pretended to be asleep but it wasn't possible. I just wanted to go home and be away from this drama.

I really didn't notice that Raquel had drunk too much. I had never heard of an alcoholic and didn't know what that was, even at 15. There was so much I didn't know. I noticed that she would have a glass of wine every now and then at home or while she was cooking either for us or for a catering party. Even in my own family, I didn't know that Dad drank too much and was probably an alcoholic and that Mom had a gambling addiction until James mentioned it when we were adults. It was sort of like, "Wow, that's right!" Come to think about, Dad really could put quite a few beers away. By that time, I had heard of those terms, like alcoholic and gambling addiction but never attributed them to my parents. It was other people, like the ones I saw on TV but not my parents. It wasn't until I read a book called, "Adult Children of Abusive Parents," that a church member told me about, that I realized that I grew up in a dysfunctional home.

So perhaps Raquel's children were blaming her for their difficult childhood or for the divorce between Raquel and her ex-husband, whom I never saw or met. Raquel never talked about her ex-husband and there weren't any pictures of him around the house to see what he looked liked. Needless to say, that was one long night and I couldn't wait to go home, which we did the next day.

Later, when Raquel asked me what I thought about the vacation, of course I said I had a good time at Disneyland and Universal Studios. Perhaps she was probing me to see what I might say to the social worker who would come and check in on me. Although I didn't say anything about the big argument she had with her children, I did make the mistake of mentioning how Andrew's house wasn't very clean and that it made me feel uncomfortable stepping out of the shower onto the dirty floor. Raquel was defensive naturally and agreed that it wasn't as clean as she would have liked it to be either but at least it was a place to stay and we didn't have to pay to sleep somewhere else. I guess sometimes, I can be a little too honest.

What I learned from that vacation and that experience is that it's not the destination that is important, it's who you are traveling with that makes you happy and brings you joy. And it's who you are with on the ride or journey. It doesn't matter if you are going on an elaborate vacation and spending a lot of money if you are with people who make you miserable and uncomfortable. I decided that I never wanted to go somewhere again unless it was with people I wanted to be with.

What I also learned was that even in Raquel's family, there were problems, conflicts, and secrets. I had no idea that other families would have problems too, especially foster families. I somehow naively thought that the foster parents or the foster family would be more stable, that they would all get along and be happy. Even though I wasn't being beaten, I still felt sad and disappointed at times that I didn't feel the love and affection that I thought I would receive from a foster family. I began to wonder if the happy families that I would see on TV ever existed.

Then, I began to miss home, as violent and painful as it was. It was strange. What and who I really missed were my two younger brothers and I missed them terribly. My love and desire to be with my brothers overshadowed any painful experiences I had with my mother. Besides, I was 16 now and hoped that things could be different between us, since three years had gone by without her seeing me or even talking to me on the phone. Perhaps she would appreciate and miss what she had. So I spoke to my social worker about returning home on the condition that I could still go to the church I had been attending. It was humbling to do that but I had seen enough drama at Raquel's and the other foster homes that I didn't feel things would get much better. So my parents were notified of my desire to come home and they agreed to have me home as well.

# 15 My Brothers' Keeper

When I returned home, things were more peaceful but awkward between Mom and me. It was peaceful at least for a little while. She had lost a lot of the excess weight caused by all the medications she had taken and no longer had the "moon face." I, on the other hand, had put on a few pounds, which I believe was from the cafeteria food that I ate from school and more American foods that I ate in the foster homes. Because we couldn't afford to buy lunch, I received food vouchers and ate at the cafeteria every day. Most of the time, the food was very fattening and greasy like lasagna, pasta, and pizza. Every now and then, I'd get a box lunch that consisted of a hamburger, fries and a soda. While I enjoyed eating those foods, I hadn't realized that they were causing me to gain weight. I had never had a weight issue before but couldn't go off grounds like some of the other kids and we couldn't bring our own lunch because my parents didn't have the money to have us make our own lunches.

Soon my brothers began to tease me for being chubby whereas before, they called me a toothpick. Now they called me a cow although I was only ten or fifteen pounds more than I was before. Mom began to say to me that when she was my age, she was never that heavy. I didn't like the way I was fitting into my clothes either and fortunately, I made most of them except for jeans or pants. But I didn't know what was causing me to put on this extra weight. After I graduated high school though, the extra weight slowly came off. So I concluded that it had to be the cafeteria school meals.

My younger brother James's voice had changed so he no longer sounded like the little innocent boy that I knew. The innocent little boy that would ask me to teach him how to crochet when he would see me crochet; the one that cried at the movie Bambi when my parents took us to see it when we were younger; the one that would get sick on the big roller coaster rides at the amusement parks that Dad took us to and whom I would tease afterwards for getting sick because I thought that since he was a boy he should have been tougher than me; and the one that I would beat playing arm wrestling. He was 11 when I left home and now he was 14 and had forgotten that he had ever asked me to teach him how to crochet and many of the other conversations that we had. At the time when he asked me how to crochet, I had told him that since he was a boy, he shouldn't want to learn how to crochet. I don't know where I got that from but regretted having told him that. I decided later that if anyone is curious about learning how to do anything, they shouldn't be disallowed to do it just because of their gender. I also came to realize that what he was really asking was to do something with his sister. He just wanted to spend some time with me since my parents were always gone.

Now he had a girlfriend, which I thought he was too young to have. I expected him to be more level-headed than that and not get involved with a girl. It made me wonder if my brothers felt like I abandoned them when I left home since I was there for them more than Mom was. I guess I didn't think about them when I ran away from home. I could only think of my own safety and my own survival that day. And when I told my social worker about what Mom had done to me when I broke the glass at the restaurant, again, I was only thinking of myself. I hadn't thought about whether my brothers would miss me or not. Somehow, I thought they'd be okay. They didn't get it as hard from Mom like I did.

Luc's English had improved quite a bit and soon he began to claim that he had forgotten a lot of the Vietnamese language. I didn't quite believe him and thought he just wanted to be like James and me who didn't know it at all, which on the one hand I could understand where he was coming from. He was left in Vietnam and for all I know, we were the spoiled kids that got to leave with Mom and Dad. Yet on the other hand, I didn't. Yes, I was ashamed of Mom's culture and didn't want anything to do with her and therefore was quite proud that I didn't know Vietnamese. However, on the other hand, I would've liked to have known what he and Mom were talking about when they would speak in Vietnamese or when she spoke with her friends.

Dennis was five when I left and was eight now and I guess he was too young to comprehend what had occurred. I hoped that was the case. However, even though he seemed to have received the most love and affection from my parents, it seemed that nobody was exempt from Mom's wrath. Since I was gone for three years, Mom had to actually take on the role of being the "mom". Since my brothers didn't know how to cook or clean the house, I would imagine she had to be home more to do the cooking and cleaning. Fortunately, maintaining a clean house was very important to her. But while she was home more, what did she do? I could only imagine because none of my brothers ever talked about what their lives were like when I was gone. Perhaps that was because Dad never talked about his feelings or displayed very many emotions. The only time I ever saw Dad cry was when his parents in Germany, my grandparents, had died. Other than that, he just stuffed his emotions and took the path of least resistance.

So even though Dennis appeared to be less affected by the dysfunction and turmoil caused by Mom's behavior, little did I know that there was something brewing inside of him. One day, after I had been living back home for about a year, I had asked Dennis to do something. I don't recall what I had asked him to do. It may have been to do his homework. Since he was the youngest, he really didn't have any chores around the house. However, his reaction to my request was quite shocking. Dennis began to get upset and started to come at me as if he wanted to fight. As I tried to defend myself and even tried to get away from him, he kept coming after me with his fists clenched and swinging his arms at me. I couldn't believe what was going on. I kept pushing him away and after several minutes, I realized that he was trying to beat me up! As he was hitting me, he kept yelling, "aaahg!" It got to the point where we were both in tears because I couldn't believe I was having a physical altercation with my ten-year-old brother! We never had any conflict before and if anything, I wanted to shield him from all the negativity around us. As he continued to strike at me with his clenched fists, I tried not to show how hurt I was or let him think that he had defeated me. Finally, after what seemed like an hour, he stopped. He had reached the point of exhaustion. Afterward, I went into my parents' room, sat on their bed and cried. I was heartbroken. Where did all this anger come from? Although I'll never know what triggered him to react so violently towards me, I'm sure it's not anything he would remember. After that incident, we never talked about what happened and I've never brought it up to him since.

Because I had been gone for three years, my canopy bedroom set was sold and Luc was moved into my room. So I had to sleep on the couch in the living room. Then, when I wanted to go to sleep, I would have to endure the noise from the TV, my parents and brothers if they were still up watching TV. Most of the time I didn't mind but sometimes, they would be watching shows like Benny Hill that often depicted nudity in their skits. According to the church I was attending, shows like that were not recommended to be watched and I was surprised that Mom would watch a show like that since she was such a devout Catholic. Sometimes I would try to stay up and watch the show with my family and saw at times there were some pretty funny skits but when they began to show the nudity, I would turn around and face the back of the couch as I was lying down.

Now that I was back home, it didn't take long before I fell back into the role of the surrogate mother again. However, since I was now 16, I was okay with it because I loved my brothers so much. I felt so sorry for them that we had a mother like we did and I realized that if I didn't do it, then who would? Soon, I was cooking, doing the laundry, vacuuming, cleaning the bathroom, dusting, helping my two younger brothers with their homework, along with doing mine, and cutting my two younger brother's hair. I had learned to cut hair from a book that showed you how to do home haircuts. My brother James loved getting his hair cut and about every four weeks, he wanted me to cut his hair, which grew out quickly.

I would often say, "But I just cut it not too long ago."

He would beg, "I know, but my hair grows so fast. I want it cut again. This time, I want it cut ...."

He would have me do a different style almost each time. In the beginning it was fun but after a while, it became like all the other chores I was doing. I don't think my parents knew I was doing this. They never thought to think that they hadn't taken my younger brothers to the barber shop in a long time. If they did know, they never said anything. I realized that I was saving my parents a lot of money and became a little resentful that they never acknowledged me for cutting my younger brothers' hair.

Because I was doing almost all the cooking, I decided that I wanted to try out different American dishes and recipes. My parents had bought a cook book from someone who was selling them door to door so I figured that since I was doing the cooking, why shouldn't I be able to cook what I wanted? So I began asking my parents to buy different ingredients for me to cook from the cook book. To my surprise, they began to buy the ingredients I had asked for. My brothers came to really enjoy the dishes I was making, although it wasn't too hard to please three growing boys. Then James began asking me questions while I was cooking so I started to show him how to cook.

Now that James was older, he got to leave the house with his friends, some of whom had cars. Because of his friends, he was able to learn how to drive from them, even though he wasn't old enough to get a driver's permit. And because of his friends having cars, James would often go hunting and fishing in areas farther away from our neighborhood, even though we lived near a creek where he would go fishing before.

James loved hunting and fishing and would bring home all kinds of animals and creatures. James had brought home a variety of live fowl such as chicken, pheasants, ducks and white geese, which I discovered were really mean. When I did the laundry, I had to hang them out to dry in our back yard. However, with the white geese around, I had to strategically plan when I would go out to hang the laundry or pick them up from the line once they were dry. If the white geese were hanging around close to the clothing line, I wouldn't go out for fear they would attack me, which they had done before. They would honk and run towards me in an attempt to bite me. It made it very tricky to do laundry while those white geese were back there. Fortunately, we had a pretty big back yard and so if they were further away from the clothes line, I could make a quick run to hang the laundry up or take it down.

When James brought chicken home, he made a homemade chicken coop with metal net for the fencing and wood boards for the roof. The thing I learned about chickens is that they were one of the dirtiest animals. Dad told me that they would eat things that pigs wouldn't eat. Every now and then we would get an egg from one of the hens, which I would use in the cooking. Besides the different fowl animals, James brought home a rabbit, crawdads and fish that we would cook and eat, and one time, he brought home a giant toad. I will never forget the day when he brought home the biggest toad I had ever seen. I was walking up to the garage as I was coming home from school. The garage door was open and I saw James and a couple of his friends inside the garage. Then I saw a pail on the floor of the garage, which was not something I normally see. James looked at me and said, "Come look in this bucket." I have learned that whenever James asks me to do something, I should be very wary and cautious and probably not do what he asked. I slowed down my steps in suspicion of what he had asked me to do. "Why?" I replied. He said, "Just take a look inside the bucket."

"What's inside," I asked, as I stopped a few feet away.

"It's no big deal. Just see what I found today."

As I slowly walked closer to the pail, I finally got a glimpse of what was inside the pail. The giant toad was so big that it made me scream. I had never seen anything like it before! The toad was so big that it filled up the entire pail. There was no way it could move.

"Where did you find it?!" I asked.

"By the creek," he replied.

"What are you going to do with it?"

"I'll probably just let it loose again."

"Not around here I hope."

"No, I'll probably just take it back to the creek."

"Oh good."

Aside from that one incident with Dennis, for the most part, I got along well with my two younger brothers and pretty much ignored my older brother. James and Dennis loved to scare me since I got startled easily. They would hide in the coat closet, bathroom or one of the bedrooms when I got home from school and jump out to scare and terrorize me as I walked by. I would scream bloody murder and tell them that one of these days, they were going to give me a heart attack, to which they would laugh even harder. James would try to get me to do things just to get a reaction out of me, like putting my tongue on a battery and tell me that it wouldn't hurt. Even though I was quite gullible, I never fell for that one. James's friends would come over and we would banter back and forth. I was quite witty and was proud of it but I also had a very sharp tongue and could cut up his friends into pieces.

One time, a neighbor kid came over and I said something to him about being a "honky". I don't know what possessed me to say what I did since he hadn't done anything or said anything to hurt me. I was surprised by the reaction I received from him, which he basically indicated that I had hurt his feelings and that I wasn't being fair to him. He said calmly, "I didn't come over to cause any trouble or to call you names." I realized after that, that I needed to be more careful about my humor and bantering. I also realized that in a way, I wanted to get to him before he had gotten to me. I guess I had misjudged him and already had my defenses up since I was considered the minority in the neighborhood. Even though James and Dennis were half Vietnamese, neither one of them looked it so they were able to pass off for being Caucasian. However, I wasn't, so I subconsciously felt that I had to justify my existence.

Nevertheless, the bantering, joking around, and repartees with my brother's friends won a lot of points with them and I began to suspect that several of them had crushes on me. A couple of them even wanted to date me but I couldn't imagine dating anyone my age or someone that was my brother's age. Later, I found out from James that they all had crushes on me, even the ones I didn't think did. But I wanted to be with someone who was older and more mature. After all, I had to grow up fast because of all the responsibilities that were heaped upon me at such a young age. I had all the responsibilities of an adult but none of the control, and I had no voice. This gave me the feelings of extreme and intense pressure of having to care for my brothers and even Dad.

As I had stipulated for my return home, I was able to go to the church I had been going to while my parents took my brothers to Mass every Sunday. Different friends from the church would come pick me up and then take me home afterwards. I also wanted to continue my weekly Bible studies but didn't tell my parents about it. It was enough that I was now going to a different church than they were. Now I was studying with Mary Jane who lived in a neighborhood across the high school I attended. She was about 13 years older than me and even though she wasn't old enough to be my mother, I looked up to her as my mentor. Mary Jane was married to Robert, who was a 6'4" tall Mexican American man, while Mary Jane was not quite 5'3" and had big blue eyes with frosted blond hair.

So once a week, I would walk over to Robert and Mary Jane's house to have my weekly Bible study. I really liked Mary Jane. She was easy to talk to and we had a lot in common although I didn't know that for quite some time. Mary Jane and Robert were a very private couple and didn't share very much with me and other people. Gradually, I learned that Mary Jane grew up in a very dysfunctional home as well and that was why she could relate to Lori and me. Lori was also having weekly Bible studies with Mary Jane but on a different day.

It was so easy to talk to Mary Jane about the difficult relationship I had with Mom. Mary Jane was the oldest of five children and all her younger siblings were her half siblings since her mother and biological father had divorced when she was very young. So she had to take care of her younger siblings while her mother and stepfather worked. Her mother relied a lot on Mary Jane and even though her mother didn't physically abuse her, Mary Jane had a lot of responsibilities like I did. Unlike my mother, Mary Jane's mother would tell her how she was a good child and commended her for doing such a good job with taking care of her younger siblings. Her mother would also tell Mary Jane that she loved her. Mary Jane confided in me that when her mother did that, it made her confused because her mother would say one thing but then her behavior was inconsistent with the things that she said. Both her mother and stepfather had drinking problems and she would see her stepfather being physically abusive to her mother. She told me that Mom did me a favor by telling me things that were consistent with her behavior. Because I didn't understand what Mary Jane meant, I didn't know what to say in response. In my mind, I thought at least her mom would tell her that she loved her whereas my mom never did.

Mary Jane was studying to be a nurse before she met Robert but quit her studies after they got married. Now, she was studying to be a psychiatric technician because she had always had an interest in psychology and wanted to understand why people did what they did. Mary Jane became a housewife after she married Robert but she had a lot of skills to go along with that role. Robert and Mary Jane would buy fixer upper homes, remodel them and then sell them for a profit. I was so impressed with Robert and Mary Jane, like how they worked well as a team to flip houses. They would lay tile down on the floors and they would paint the walls of the homes. Mary Jane would sew the drapes for the windows and even reupholstered furniture. They did everything themselves and I thought when I got older, I wanted to have just as many skills and talent as Mary Jane did.

After our one hour Bible study, Mary Jane would drive me home. Most of the time Mom wasn't home but on the rare occasion that she was, she would ask me why I had gotten home late from school, to which I would explain that I had to study after school. Or I would say that I went by the mall after school, which I would because we had to pass by the mall on my way home. So, I didn't feel I was lying. I was just sort of stretching the truth a little or just omitting a few other details. As intuitive and perceptive as Mom was, I was quite surprised that she never knew I was having Bible studies. That made me feel and believe that God was looking out for me and that He really wanted me to continue my studies.

As I continued studying the Bible with Mary Jane, I became more and more comfortable in sharing my problems about Mom with her. She was the only other person I felt safe with, besides Lori, to talk about my feelings and the things that were going on at home. Mary Jane told me to start journalizing my feelings since it would be very therapeutic for me. However, I explained to her what happened with Mrs. Gray, the first foster home I lived in, how Mrs. Gray read my diary and how I felt so violated by that. So I couldn't write because I was afraid that someone would discover my journal and read what I wrote. Mary Jane said, "So what if someone reads what you wrote." However, I couldn't risk it. I couldn't risk exposing myself again. No, I would not write.

Yet when things became so stressful because of Mom, I kept thinking about what Mary Jane said about writing. So I began to do some journalizing in short hand, since I had taken a short hand class in my sophomore year of high school. I decided that if someone was to find my journals and notes, they wouldn't be able to read it because it was in short hand.

## Going Where the Money Is

I hadn't been home too long before Dad told us that he had gotten a job in Alaska. My heart sank when he told us that. The thought of him not being home to buffer some of Mom's anger was not something I was looking forward to. I felt abandoned by him. How could he leave me here with this monster of a mother? But, he was offered a well paying job as a Civil Engineer for the Navy. So while he was on Adak working, he would send money home to Mom to pay for the expenses.

Even though Dad was making more money working in Alaska, I still wasn't given any extra privileges or allowances. I was sewing and making a lot of my own clothes except for jeans from the money I had made at Raquel, which was quickly running out, so I decided to get a job. Besides, I was going to be 18 soon and wanted to make sure I had enough to live off of when I moved out on my own. Fortunately, I was able to get a job working at a yogurt shop in the mall, which was owned by one of the ministers in the congregation that I went to. I was only given part-time hours because full-time hours and benefits were only given to the manager.

Now that Dad was gone in Alaska, the tension between Mom and I began to build again. Even though she didn't physically hit me anymore, she still mentally and verbally berated me. She would give me long lectures on how displeased she was with me. Also, since Dad wasn't around to help supervise us kids, Luc and Mom began to have conflicts as well. I guess Luc felt he could get away with acting out more, now that Dad wasn't around. One time, Mom and Luc were arguing about something to the point where she began hitting him. I don't know what they were arguing about since they were talking in Vietnamese. The yelling and violence began to escalate to the point where Mom ended up calling the police on Luc. It was quite embarrassing to see the police car parked in front of our house and many of our neighbors outside, watching and wondering what was going on. I talked to the police officer briefly outside before he went into the house. For once, I was glad it didn't involve me. Unfortunately, there wasn't much he could do but to talk to them. Luke was 18 and even though he still had to finish high school, evidently, he was ready to leave home too.

As much as Mom wanted to keep me a little girl even though I had all the adult responsibilities, it was surprising that she allowed me to meet one of her friend's brother. Mom's friends Kim, who was Vietnamese, and Jason, who was Caucasian, were a young couple who lived a few minutes from our home.

Jason's younger brother Jeremy, who was almost 20 came visiting from Indiana one time and was told about me. Jeremy and his girlfriend had broken up so he came to stay with Jason and Kim for a while. One day, Mom took me with her to Jason and Kim's house where I met Jeremy, who liked me right away. As we approached Kim and Jason's house, there was a car parked in the street in front of their house with the hood up. So Mom parked across the street. After we got out of the car and walked around the parked car, we saw Jeremy in front of it. Even though I had never seen him before, I knew it was him. As we walked around him my heart began to pound. He had dark blond wavy hair with blue eyes and as he looked at me with that faraway gaze, he introduced himself. As I looked at him, I thought, where is he looking?

"Hi, I'm Jeremy," he said, "I'll be in, in a minute."

"Okay," I replied and as I continued to walk with Mom into the house.

Jeremy picked me up a few days later and took me bowling. I had only gone bowling a few times before and it had been a while. Needless to say, I bowled terribly. The ball kept going into the gutter and I felt so embarrassed, but Jeremy was kind and patient and helped me with my technique. I was nervous because not only had it been a while since I had gone bowling but also because I had never been on a date before. I was so surprised that Mom had let me go with Jeremy, especially to go alone with him.

I don't remember much more of the date except that when he dropped me off, he gave me a kiss that I will never forget. My brother James was outside with one of his friends and was just coming home from a day of fishing. I was certain they saw me and Jeremy kissing but I didn't care. I was exhausted from being so nervous and from the intense feelings of attraction and chemistry that I had never felt before. When I came into the house, I went straight into my parents' room and crashed on their bed, since I didn't want to sleep on the living room couch. After I woke up from my nap, I called my friend Lori right away and told her about my date with Jeremy. Lori told her sister Summer, who later teased me about it, but I didn't care.

Mom talked to me a few days later about Jeremy and in her own way, tried to talk to me about sex but I could tell she wasn't sure how to approach me about it. I told her that I knew what she was talking about since I had sex education in school when I was in the seventh grade. It was really awkward so I was glad we didn't talk about it again.

When I went out on the date with Jeremy and thought I might be interested in dating him, I told Mary Jane about him and asked her to study with me about dating. Mary Jane agreed but I could tell she felt awkward about it too. I couldn't understand why because she was married. Besides, if I were like her own daughter, wouldn't she have to do this anyway? Even though we started to study out of one of the books on dating, marriage, and a happy family life, it seemed as though she would keep things very general. I could tell that she was very uncomfortable talking about the subject of sex.

Throughout the approximately three years that I studied with Mary Jane and beyond, she would always tell me about the negative side of marriage. Mary Jane would tell me how it's not always a bed of roses, which I knew that it wasn't. I wasn't that naïve to think everything would be perfect after you get married. Besides, I learned that you had to be happy first before you could be happy with someone else and that you can't expect someone else to make you happy. I knew all of that and saw not only in my own family, but also in the three foster homes I lived in, that there are certainly many marriages and families who weren't happy. However, as in the cases of those within church, at least they had a better chance at happiness because of having the same values and goals in life.

Nevertheless, I would hear over and over from Mary Jane about the dismal and gloomy side of marriage and would talk about how Robert wasn't the Prince Charming she expected.

Even though she never went into details or specifics, it was enough for me to get her message. I never expressed this to her but I wondered why she kept telling me all the negative side of marriage and wondered if she really was happy in her marriage with Robert like she said she was. I would tell her that I knew all that but at least there had to be something good or positive to look forward to when it comes to marriage.

At the time, I would just listen to her say these things and not respond much because I looked up to her and knew in her own way, she was trying to look out for me. However, I grew weary of her talking to me as if I didn't know these things. I wasn't living in a fairytale world and if I really thought a marriage would save me, I could have easily found someone to get me out of the predicament I was in with my family. But I didn't, because I knew that would have been for the wrong reasons. Eventually, I became angry as I reflected on all the times that Mary Jane would tell me about the doom and gloom of marriage. I didn't realize that she too became part of my programming of painting a bleak and hopeless picture of marriage.

Later, I found out that Jeremy's former girlfriend who was around his age, had come looking for him and wanted to get back with him. She even came to stay with Kim and Jason while Jeremy was still there. When Mom was going over to visit Kim again, she asked if I wanted to go. Because Jeremy's girlfriend was there, she told me that I didn't have to go. However, I decided to go anyway. I wanted to show Jeremy that I really didn't care that he had gotten back together with his ex-girlfriend. When Mom and I arrived, it was a little awkward at first but I ended up having a private conversation with Jeremy's girlfriend, Katrina. It just sort of worked out that way where everyone else was in the living room, while she and I were in the dining room.

Katrina told me that she came from a very dysfunctional family where her father would beat her so that she didn't have very much self-esteem. Because of the abuse from her father, she ran away from home and relied on Jeremy for support but it sounded like she also relied on other guys for support as well. However, after she and Jeremy broke up, that's when she realized she really needed him and what a nice guy he was, because the other guy didn't treat her as well as he did. While I sat there and empathized with her, because I could relate to some of things she had gone through as far as having an abusive parent, I couldn't relate to how she dealt with her problems. She took up smoking, which I tried but because of positive peer pressure and things I was learning from church, I chose not to smoke. I also didn't turn to men to rely on for financial or emotional support at the sacrifice of losing my own dignity. I knew that to rely on a man or to get married to someone just because I wanted out of my problems at home was the wrong reason to get into a relationship or to get married. I had reasoned that it's not a good idea to jump from the frying pan into the fire.

I don't know how or where I gained the wisdom and maturity to reason that way but I'm glad I did. Perhaps it was from going to church and the people I associated with. Unfortunately, I wasn't always able to remain that level-headed and grew up to make many mistakes later in my life. Nevertheless, I did learn from my mistakes, which helped me to be less judgmental of others and to have more compassion for them.

As Mom and I were leaving, I overheard Jeremy tell Jason that he was happy that Katrina and I were getting along. I thought how arrogant he was to assume that I would have anything more to do with him from that point on. I also thought he was stupid to go back to her or take her back after she had left him for someone else. After that, I never saw Jeremy or Katrina again.

About a year or so later, I heard that Jeremy and Katrina were having a baby. They were not married and that was something that was not approved by God, according to what I had learned from my Bible studies and from going to church. I thought, *Wow, that could have been me.* Then I would be stuck taking care of a baby and a husband when I felt like I had already had enough of caretaking. I was thankful that I had learned the things I did from church to help me avoid making mistakes like that, as I had viewed them at the time. My faith had kept me sheltered from many things that were considered wrong in God's eyes. If I hadn't found my faith when I did, I am almost certain I would have done some of the same things Katrina did.

Jeremy and Katrina had another child but they continued to have problems. Katrina would cheat on Jeremy with the EMT's that she worked with. After about five years, he had enough and they separated. Now, Jeremy had two girls to take care of. He had asked about me but by that time, I had totally lost interest in him. I was on my own and having a good time doing things with my friends from church, like traveling, hiking, and going to concerts, so I had no interest in getting back with a guy who chose to go back to an unstable, toxic, and dysfunctional ex-girlfriend. No, I was not going to be used to take care of his girls. I had already raised my brothers practically and I was enjoying the freedom of just taking care of myself.

# 16 Driving Under the Influence of Criticism

While my friends in school were getting their driver's permit, I still didn't have mine. Now that Dad made more money, my parents decided to get a moped for my brother James and to get a bike for me. But the only place I could ride my bike was to school or work. I was still stuck at home and couldn't go anywhere else. So I begged my parents to let me get my driver's permit, which they finally did. I took a driver's education class at the school and passed with high scores, as far as the simulator goes. Then I was able to start driving but of course with an adult. The only adult available was Mom since Dad was up in Alaska, which wasn't a fun experience to endure. Every time I drove, Mom would take the opportunity to lecture me about how I was a horrible daughter.

"When I was your age, I had to work very hard," she would lecture in her broken English. I would try not to roll my eyes because if she caught me doing that, she would get angry and jump all over me so I would just look straight ahead or turn the other way. I couldn't stand to look at her. *Yes, I know how hard you had to work and I guess you have to make sure that I had it just as hard as you did. What's wrong here? First of all, we're not living in Vietnam and I would think that as a mother, you would want the best for your children, that you would want things to be better for them, especially if you only have one daughter. That's what I would have wanted. Why would you want your children's lives to be miserable, especially when you knew what that was like?* I would think to myself. If there was a cultural reason for the way she was treating me, she didn't explain it.

Then she was always telling me I didn't do something right in regards to my driving. It was constant criticism and negative comments. On and on she would go. And it was usually just her and me in the car where she would constantly criticize me.

"You drive too fast" or "You drive too slow." "You stop too far from line," or "You stop to close to line," at an intersection. "You stop too fast," or "You need to stay in middle," or "You turn too fast!" If I did anything correctly, she never mentioned it.

Looking back, I wondered if she still would have been as critical of me, or if she would have lectured me like she did if my brothers were in the car. Because somehow, it was always just her and me in the car. If we were driving for ten, fifteen, or twenty minutes, I would get lectured for that entire time. Since there was no where I could go, she would take advantage of that time. There was no escaping her indignation and clear intention to break me down.

Finally, it was time for me to get my actual license. When it came to the written test, I passed it with flying colors. However, when it came to the actual driving portion of the test, I failed. I didn't understand why at first. I knew how to drive and understood the traffic rules since I had passed the written test. I also did well with the driving simulator in driving school. But why couldn't I pass the actual driving test? I felt embarrassed and ashamed because I had never failed a test before. I considered myself pretty smart, despite what Mom said. The grades I got in school proved it and it seemed the teachers like me too.

I realized later that it was because of the constant criticism Mom inflicted on me while I was driving. I couldn't do anything right. To actually drive was nerve wracking for me. I was so stressed and uptight every time I got into the car because that was when Mom would mentally and verbally attack me.

Even though I thought I could just ignore her and drown her out, I didn't realize that the constant criticism was affecting how I felt while driving. I was a nervous wreck, constantly in fear that I was going to do something wrong and get yelled at. I guess instead of really seeing what was around me, my mind went somewhere else to try and escape the present moment in the car while Mom would go on and on with the mental and verbal bashing. At times, I was afraid she would actually hit me while I was driving in the car because of her anger.

When Dad came down from Alaska for a visit, I asked that he ride with me to see how I was doing with my driving. To my surprise, he said I did very well. Wow! What a contrast! I was expecting him to say at least one thing that I didn't do correctly since Mom was constantly telling me I wasn't doing something right. But he didn't. When we got home from the ride Dad said, "You did good."

I asked astonished, "Really?"

He said, "Yeah, you did very good."

I was tempted to tell him how Mom was relentlessly criticizing my driving but decided that it would do little good. Besides, I didn't want to ruin the good feeling I had by bringing Mom up for fear he might begin to find fault in my driving as well. So that was all I needed. I just needed somebody to tell me that I was doing okay with my driving. And I was glad that it was Dad that told me that.

When Dad pointed out how well I did with my driving, it reminded me of how he used to be. When he was more calm, reasonable, and less stressed about things. I began to notice that Dad seemed much more relaxed during his visit. The financial stress was no longer looming over his head since the job in Alaska paid quite well. Also, he had been away from the chaos, drama, and dysfunction of the family life created by Mom.

Despite Mom's constant criticism of me while I was driving, I finally passed the driving test but not without an incident. During the second go around, I did something that I thought would cause me to not pass the test again. I didn't do anything wrong, I just went over a deep ditch in a road too fast. I was the first to drive when the driving instructor took me and two other potential licensees out to test our driving. I was driving through a neighborhood by the freshmen high school with the driving instructor sitting in the passenger's seat and the two other driving students sitting in the back seat. Although I went to that high school for my freshman year, I had never walked around the neighborhood so I was unfamiliar with the area. It was a quiet neighborhood with lots of big trees, which created a lot of shading. The homes were older but nice and they were all different from each other.

As I was driving along within the speed limit through the neighborhood, I approached an intersection that had a deep dip in the road prior to entering the intersection. Because I didn't know about the ditch and didn't anticipate it, I didn't slow down as I approached it. I ended up driving through the dip so fast that after coming out of it, the car bounced up high. As the car was bouncing up out of the ditch, I happened to look into the rear view mirror and saw that the two students in the back seat had bounced off their seats, which made me laugh hysterically. I don't know why I thought it was so funny but what made it funnier was seeing the wide-eyed petrified looks on their faces. I was laughing so hard that I thought I would have to pull over. Then I looked over at the driving instructor and saw that he wasn't laughing either and his face looked somewhat tensed. I finally realized that I was the only one laughing. I obviously never drove in that neighborhood before and told the instructor that. Then I silently prayed that he wouldn't take off any points for that incident. Needless to say, I passed but barely. Still, I was so relieved. I had finally gotten my license.

When my family moved to Alaska, I was left with the family car, an olive green Ford Pinto station wagon with wood grain panel on the side. While I was thankful that my parents left me the car, it wasn't exactly the type of car that I would've chosen. Not only was it not a "cool" car to be driving, it was also having mechanical problems. So Dad told me to take it to a neighbor, who was a mechanic.

The Stevens were an African American family with two girls and one boy. Their oldest daughter was already living on her own so I became friends with Gina, and James became friends with Wesley. Mr. Stevens, their father, agreed to work on the car again. He had worked on it before when Dad was working up in Alaska. It was convenient to take it to Mr. Stevens because he worked on it in his home driveway, which was only three houses down from me.

However, Mr. Stevens was gone a lot so the car sat in his driveway for weeks. Every now and then I would check with Mrs. Stevens to see how Mr. Stevens was doing with the car since I needed it to drive to work. Fortunately I had my bike to ride to work at the yogurt shop, which wasn't too far from my house. But I preferred driving since it was faster. Also, I wanted to drive myself to church instead of having someone else pick me up. However, after about the third time I came over to check on the car, Mrs. Stevens got really angry at me. "He'll get to it when in can!" she yelled. I had never seen Mrs. Stevens get upset like that before, let alone get upset at me. I needed my car, especially if I was going to be moving and getting another job that was going to be further away than where I lived. I later learned from Dad that Mr. Stevens had a drinking problem and that's probably why he didn't always want to work. As the time came close for the new renters of my parents' house to move in, Mr. Stevens managed to get the car running.

I drove the car around for a little longer until it began to have problems again. It began to run really slow and even if I pressed the accelerator all the way to the floor, it wouldn't go over 10 or 15 miles per hour. One morning, as I was driving to work, the car suddenly went into slow mode. I was going along a street in the neighborhood and a car approached me from behind. I felt really embarrassed because my car was going so slow and I didn't want to detain the driver behind me, so I rolled down the window and waved him to pass me up. I then realized that I *had* to get a new car. After a while, the car stopped running completely. Fortunately, it was parked at the house where I was living at the time. I finally ended up selling it to a mechanic for $100. I later learned that he was able to get it up and running again. However, I didn't care. I was so done with that embarrassing and uncool car.

After that, I bought a used 1969 VW Beetle. It was light blue and had "Think Bug" pinstriped along the bottom of each side of the car. The driver's license frame said, "Hairdressers do it with style." I thought it was so cool and told my friends, "Hey, isn't that a neat saying? You know, 'Hairdressers, Style.' Get it?" My friends would say, "Um, I don't think it means what you think it does. And I don't think you should have it on your car."

"What do you mean?" I asked naively. But my friends wouldn't explain it to me so it took me a while to "get it". Since I was trained to do the "right" thing all the time and to be obedient, I didn't question it any further and had it removed.

## 17 Almost Homeless But Someone Is Watching Over Me

After about a year and a half living up in Adak by himself, Dad decided to have the family move up there. Even though he never admitted it, I knew he got lonely up there. After seeing the pictures that he had taken of Adak, I could see why. There were no trees on the island, only a few shrubs and bushes. There was nothing but the naval air station and aside from working, fishing, and hunting, there wasn't much else to do up there. I don't know if he and Mom decided to wait for me and Luc to graduate from high school or it just worked out that way. The news about having the family move up to Adak was somewhat a relief. Finally, I could be on my own and get away from my crazy mother and all the responsibilities of caring for my brothers. As much as I loved them, I was ready to move on with my own life and do the things I wanted to do instead of having the burden of taking care of a family.

Despite not knowing where I was going to live or what I was going to do for work, I knew I didn't want to move to Adak. There was no way Mom and I could survive living on a small remote island. I was certain we would tear each other apart. Besides, what would I do up there? There wasn't a college for me to attend and even if there was, I didn't think I could attend because Dad said he wasn't going to pay for it. However, it did make me feel good that Dad bought a ticket for me to go just in case. It helped to lessen the feeling of abandonment. I was ready to fly and to be on my own. I was making friends at church and felt like I had a sense of belonging and acceptance so I just trusted that things would work out. My desire to be on my own and to get away from my family was stronger than my fear of being alone and not knowing where I was going to live or how I was going to support myself. I just kept imagining the feeling of freedom.

Since I was only working part-time at the yogurt shop, I told the owner that I needed full-time hours so I could support myself without my family. Brian, the owner, told me that he would give me full-time hours but as the time got closer to my family moving, he still hadn't done it. After reminding him a couple more times, Brian still wouldn't give me full-time hours, which confused me because he knew of my situation and also because he was one of the ministers in the church. I thought the ministers were supposed to help those in the congregation. Evidently, I was wrong. I soon realized that he never intended to give me full-time hours, even though he said he would. I was disappointed but I didn't have time to stay disappointed. I had to find a full-time job and I had to find one fast. So I went to a temp agency that found me a full-time position working as a cashier in a local family owned gift and stationary store.

After my family moved out, I lived at the house for about one month. The day they left was one of the saddest days of my life. How was that possible? Even though I was glad to have my family move away, I didn't expect to feel so sad about it. With all the furniture gone except for my bed, Luc's black and white TV, and a small old vintage sofa made of all wood frame with orange cushioned seating and backing, it left an eerie and empty feeling inside. As I walked through the rooms, especially my brother's room, I could hear their voices. I cried for days in shock and sadness for what I thought would be the happiest and most liberating days of my life, but what turned out to be so empty and hollow. I felt confused. How can I feel so sad for and miss something that made me feel so angry, depressed, and suffocating? The anger and hate from Mom was so toxic and poisonous and the responsibilities of having to be the mother to my three brothers made me feel as if I was confined to a prison. I felt restricted, like I couldn't breathe. I was certainly taken advantage of and taken for granted since there was *never* any thanks for all that I had done. How can I miss and feel sad for those things? It was mainly my two younger brothers that I missed and whom I cried for the most. It was *their* voices that I kept hearing as I walked through the house.

Thankfully, I did have Pepper, our little Peekapoo dog. Out of the two dogs that we had, Pepper was the cutest, friendliest, and sweetest dog. Her fur was a mix of gray, white and black so that's why we named her Pepper. She was no more than ten pounds and had a lot of energy. She also had an amazing disposition. She was always happy, and loved to run around and play with the neighborhood kids. When we got her as a puppy, she was initially allowed in the house but when everyone was gone, she would chew up the furniture. We'd come home to chewed up furniture legs and holes in the sofa cushions with the inside fibers and contents of the cushion seats strewn all over the floor. Interestingly, as destructive as Pepper was, my parents didn't get too angry or upset with her. She was the family's first puppy and admittedly, she was very cute. After several days of destruction, they decided to have her stay in the garage during the day when nobody was home. That was where she would sleep as well.

Pepper was definitely an outdoor dog and was always outside running in the yard either chasing or being chased by my brothers, a neighbor kid, or another dog. One summer she had rolled around so much on the grass that she ended up getting a lot of pinwheel-like seeds that come from a lawn weed stuck in her fur. These seed pods initially are green and are shaped like tiny flat snails with tiny spikes all over but once they become dry, they would turn brown and stick like velcro to just about anything. She had literally hundreds of these tiny pinwheel stickers in her fur that pulled on it and made it so matted that I had to cut them out of her. I recall sitting in the garage with a pair of scissors and cutting these little pinwheel stickers out of her fur. The task was so tedious but I knew she had to be so uncomfortable, especially if she was to lie down. Certainly these little spikes would poke through her fur and prick her skin. As she laid on the concrete floor, I kept cutting and cutting and cutting. The garage door was open and James, who had been out playing with friends, came to check on what I was doing. He hadn't realized that Pepper had these prickly seeds all over her. Nobody else noticed it either. After I was satisfied that I had gotten all of the seeds out of her fur, three hours had gone by. Afterwards, I gave her a bath. She may not have looked like the best groomed dog but at least I knew she would be much more comfortable. After that, I made sure to check her fur more frequently and remove the prickly seeds before too many of them got stuck to her again.

Sadly, when I moved out of my parents' house, I couldn't take Pepper with me. I could barely take care of myself, let alone another animal, even if she was just another small mouth to feed. So Dad arranged for Dino, a retired widower that lived two houses from us to have Pepper. Dino was a short and stout Italian man and his wife, who was Japanese, had died many years ago. His two daughters were grown and living on their own. I only remember seeing one of the daughters who would come and visit Dino every now and then. Dino came across as a grumpy old man and mostly kept to himself. His front yard had a wooden fence around it and if a ball accidentally got into his yard while the neighbor kids were playing some kind of sport, he would come out and start yelling at the kids. Every now and then, you would see him out in his front yard doing yard work or watering the lawn, but instead of thinking he was mean, I just felt sorry for him. I knew he must have been lonely living by himself. So when I gave Pepper to him, I knew she was the best thing that could have happened to him. I heard from Dad that he really loved Pepper and took very good care of her.

The other family dog we had was Spunky who was also a mixed breed, but we didn't know of what. To me he looked like a mix between a Lab and a Wiener dog. He had the coloring of a tan lab but he had short legs and a thick and stocky body. Spunky seemed to be a pretty mild and even keeled dog but at times, he certainly lived up to his name. He disliked anyone in a uniform like many dogs, and barked ferociously if the mailman or anyone in a uniform approached the house. Even with certain strangers, Spunky would become hostile. Once, while Spunky was out in the garage with my brothers and his friends, a man approached the house. For some reason Spunky didn't like or trust this man so he bit the man in the butt. It wasn't severe but it let us know that we had to keep an eye on him.

Since we didn't get Spunky as a puppy, we didn't know if he was fixed or not. However, whenever another dog in the neighborhood went into heat, Spunky would crawl through a hole in the fence he had dug and run away. We never could find the hole and at times, I thought he jumped over the fence, which seemed impossible when you look at his stocky legs and thick body. The fence was five feet high, but since we didn't know where the hole was, that was the only explanation that I could find to explain how he got out. Later, Dad told me that he indeed escape through a hole in the fence. Each time he ran away, my brother James, with the help of one of his friends, would find him. Sometimes, they would find him in another neighbor's backyard. Even though Spunky wasn't any special breed, people liked him and would have kept him if James hadn't found him. One time, when James brought Spunky back from running away, I noticed that his coat and fur looked shinier and healthier. We concluded that the family he was temporarily with had fed him fish or some other rich type of food that would affect his coat that way.

"So you think life would be better living with another family don't you?" I asked him.

As soon as I said that, he turned his head away from me. I knew that he knew what I was saying. It was if he was too good for us.

"I can't believe this! You're trying to ignore me?" I said chuckling. "Well!"

Another time he ran away, Dad found him almost ten miles out of town. As Dad was driving along the freeway between Merced and Castle AFB, he saw Spunky running along the highway. Where he was going, we had no idea. Sadly, one day Spunky ran away again and this time, my brother James couldn't find him. It seemed he just couldn't hang with us. Either he wanted to live in greener pastures or he just wanted to find his previous home.

**Abandoned Once Again**

As if my family moving away, having to quickly find a full-time job, and then look for a place to live wasn't enough, my best friend Lori and her family decided to move to Las Vegas. I couldn't understand why she would want to move away and it made me feel sad. I thought she would have wanted to be on her own since she was the oldest and had most of the responsibilities too. However, I came to realize that it was still much different for her. One, her mother never beat her and she had a sister that was two years younger than her that also helped out. There were three of them as far as children goes and there were four of us, except I had to care for everyone. Lori was also more dependent on her family and really loved her mom and her sisters. Even though her mother didn't verbally abuse her, she did pick up some negative thoughts about herself for she would often say, "I have three things against me. My faith, I'm a female, and I'm black."

I couldn't understand why she would say those things because I thought, *Well, I'm a female too and I'm a minority as well in this town. So what? Look at Oprah. She's black and she is very successful. And what about the black news reporters I would see on TV. They didn't let their color keep them from being successful.* So I would tell her those things and she would agree but she still didn't believe that she could achieve those things. After hearing her say those negative things about herself too many times I became annoyed with her. However, I realized that the only person she could've possibly gotten those ideas from was her mother.

Lori and I were both 18 now and according to Dad, every one of his siblings left home when they were 18. That's how it was in Germany, according to Dad. However, although he was the youngest of the siblings, he was the first to leave home at age 14 when he joined the Merchant Marines. Since Dad had to leave home at a young age, he would tell us kids that we had to be on our own too once we turned 18. Nevertheless, it didn't all work out that way since Luc was almost twenty when we graduated because he was two years older than me. Whereas, I was only 17 ½ when I graduated high school. And even though I was 18 when my family moved away, Dad did buy a ticket for me to move with them to Alaska in case I changed my mind.

It was spring time when my family moved away and even though we lived in what used to be a dessert, there was still more rain to come. A storm had come in through the night as I lay in my bed in the fetal position trying to sleep. I was alone in the house. There were no brothers sleeping in the room next to me and no parents in the room across the hall. The wind was howling loudly and ruthlessly as it smashed and whipped the leaves and branches of the bushes against my bedroom window. The shadows of the leaves and branches of the bushes looked like giant disfigured fingers and heads. No, I will not let my imagination get the best of me. Aside from the heavy rain drops and bushes banging against my window, I heard some other noises. Were they from inside the house? What was that? I lay alert, waiting. Then I began to have this creepy feeling all over my body as if someone else was in the house. As if I was no longer alone. I lay still, trying not to move or breathe, just in case there was someone in the house and watching me, I didn't want them to think I was awake. I gripped my blanket tightly around me and made sure everything except my head was covered. The feeling grew and soon, it felt as if someone was in my room. I held my breath and laid still, paralyzed in fear. For how long, I don't recall. Slowly, the feeling went away and I realized that I may have let my imagination go too far. I needed to get some sleep because I had to go work at the yogurt shop tomorrow.

When I awoke, the storm had passed and all was quiet. It was still a little overcast but the rain had stopped. I got up as usual with just enough time to get ready to go to work. I went to open the house door to the garage and saw that the garage door was swung wide open. Pepper was in the garage and as soon as she saw me, she walked towards me with her tail wagging to greet me. That's strange. Was the wind *that* powerful last night that it would swing the garage door open? Ever since we moved into that neighborhood, we had never locked the garage door, even though there was a lock on it. It had been a relatively safe neighborhood and we never had any problems with burglary or theft. Oh well, I didn't have time to think about it anymore, I had to get to work. So after pulling my bike out, I closed the garage door without locking it and rode my bike to the mall where the yogurt shop was.

After my four hour shift was over, I rode home. It was still daylight. Then, as I walked through the kitchen, I noticed something was different. Something was missing. Trent, one of my brother's friends had loaned me his boom box. I had left it on the kitchen counter and now it was gone. What? Wait a minute. Then, I went into the living room and Luc's black and white TV that had been lying on the floor was gone too! What?! As I walked through the rest of the house, I discovered that the medium sized suitcase that was in my bedroom closet, the same suitcase my parents had bought to put my clothes in and delivered to me when I was placed in the receiving home was gone! How did that happen? So that creepy feeling I had last night that someone was in my bedroom, you mean someone actually *was* in my bedroom?! Ahhhh! How come I didn't notice these things missing this morning!? I no longer felt safe. I called Dad up in Alaska to tell him what happened. He told me to report it to the insurance company and gave me all the information to do so.

When I called the insurance company to let them know what happened, they had me fill out a form and list all the items that were missing and how old they were. I didn't know anything about depreciation and deductible so I filled it out as honestly as I could. Then, after they took off the deductible and the depreciation for each item, even though as in the suit case it was practically brand new since it was only used once, I received $20. I also had informed my brother's friend Trent about the burglary and he seemed fine at first. I told him that I had filed a claim with the insurance company.

Trent was an African American kid who lived in our neighborhood. He was tall, thin, wore glasses, and seemed pretty easy going. When I received the $20, I decided to just give it all to Trent. However, Trent was not satisfied with just the $20. He told me that the boom box cost more than that and he wanted to buy himself another one. However, with me working only part-time at the yogurt shop, there was no way I could pay him more. I was barely making it myself and needed money for food, gas, and to get into an apartment since the renters were going to be moving into the house in a few weeks. Even though I explained that to Trent, he still became upset and kept trying to get me to pay him more. As bad as I felt about not having more to give him, I simply couldn't do it. I didn't like that this happened and that it had to involve my brother's friend but there was simply not much I could do.

After the robbery, I told some of my neighbors about what happened. I also started locking the garage door with the padlock that had always been there but was never locked. I learned from my neighbors that when a certain family moved into a house across the street from my parents' house, the homes on the left side and the right side of that new family's house were robbed. Coincidence? I didn't think so. I felt angry when I heard that. I also knew that someone from that house had to have been the one who came into my home that night to strip me of what little I had, but of course, I couldn't prove it. The only people that knew of my situation were the people in the neighborhood and obviously that family had watched my parents move out. They must have also watched the neighbors on either side of them and knew when they wouldn't be home. Everyone on that street was pretty nice and even though some couples living on our street didn't have any children, they were nice people who minded their own business. So now these newbies decided to disrupt all that? Sickening.

Nevertheless, I had to focus on finding a new place. Mary Jane began taking me around to look for a new place and even though I had gotten a full-time job at the stationary store, it wasn't enough for me to find a decent place to live. Based on how much I made, we went to look at some places that weren't exactly in the best neighborhoods. Some of them were not very well kept as in the exterior needed to be painted and there was litter all around. But for me, I thought that it was at least a roof over my head. After we would leave many of those lower income apartments, which I didn't realize they were considered lower income, Mary Jane would say to me, "I think you can do better than that." I thought to myself, *If I had more money, then I could, but this is what my budget is allowing.* However, I didn't say anything to her.

Several of the friends in the congregation knew of my situation and some of them began to wonder why Mary Jane and Robert didn't take me in, especially since they were my mentors and Mary Jane was my Bible teacher. They lived in a nice, three bedroom home in a nice neighborhood so at least by appearance, they seemed to be doing well. However, Mary Jane would occasionally make the comment, "If I was rich...," so I would interpret that as her trying to tell me that they really didn't have that much money.

She would also tell me that she didn't feel understood by most people, even in church, and there weren't many people whom she could confide in. She and Robert were very private and I couldn't understand why at first. However, as I became older, I began to understand why they were. First, I came to realize that that's just some people's nature. They were private also because she came from a very dysfunctional upbringing like I did. Although she was not abused physically, she did see her stepfather being physically abusive towards her mother. So I found myself as an adult also being less divulging of my background and of my past. It was because I was ashamed of it and I knew that was how Mary Jane felt as well.

Just like my friends in school who didn't believe me when I revealed to them about how Mom beat me, most people who had a somewhat "normal" childhood are unable to relate to the abusive and dysfunctional upbringing of others. Just like I couldn't relate to others when I would hear them talk about how they went to the prom, how they played a certain instrument in school, how they played a certain sport, or how they were a cheerleader, I would often just sit quietly because I couldn't relate to what they were saying. I was too ashamed to tell them how I was confined to my home like a prisoner and had to cook, clean, and take care of my brothers and father and even with doing all of that, I was still beaten by my mother.

When I told Mary Jane about what another member in the congregation said, without divulging their name, about how they were surprised that she and Robert hadn't considered taking me in and letting me live with them, even on a temporary basis, she told me that they had considered it. However, they felt that they didn't think I would be satisfied with everything that they had to offer. She told me that I would eventually become dissatisfied with them and so they thought it would be best that I found my own place. When she told me this, I was confused. What would I become dissatisfied with? I wasn't looking for perfection. If anything, I thought their home always looked perfect. I just wanted to feel safe and to feel loved. But her explanation made me feel as if they didn't trust me and that I wasn't good enough for them to come live with them.

At the same time, Mary Jane would tell me that she loved me like I was her own child and as if she had given birth to me herself. She would also say how I was a lot like Robert, her husband, in that I was very adventurous, I would get bored easily, and was always looking for the next challenge. So this made it even more confusing because I thought that if I was like her own child, then I would think that she would allow her own child stay and live with them. Since I really loved Mary Jane and Robert, looked up to them and believed and trusted everything they told me, I just went along with what she said. It's not like I really had a choice.

I could see though, why others in the congregation thought that Mary Jane and Robert would be in the best position to offer me a place to stay until I could get my own place. They had a nice home and everything was always picture perfect. Mary Jane had decorated their home and arranged it to look like something you would see in a magazine, although some of her colors and fabrics were certainly not the popular trends of the time. Mary Jane had her own style and stuck to what she liked, no matter what the latest fad in décor was. She would paint the walls mustard yellow and used a lot of dark green in the upholstery and drapes that dressed the windows.

When I would come into their home for my weekly Bible study or just drop by for a visit after my family moved away, I was always careful when I would sit on the furniture because I didn't want to mess anything up. Even though they were always warm and inviting, there was always that feeling that you didn't want to move things around.

When it came to generosity, I began to observe in people that it seemed like sometimes the ones who don't have very much end up being some of the most kind and generous people, and the ones that have more, are less inclined to extend themselves and help others. It seemed ironic that I saw people who had plenty, which I felt Mary Jane and Robert did, were less inclined to help others in a physical or material way. They were certainly there to say the right things at the right time, especially Mary Jane. It appeared that she had inherited that gift from her mother of saying just the right words to make a person feel better. I'm sure she meant to be sincere but it seemed a bit cruel to say to a young person who has been through so much that they are loved as if they were their own child, but then turn them away when they needed help.

Mary Jane and I continued to drive around to places that were affordable for me, but we just couldn't find anything. So I talked to Dad and he gave me the phone number of the renters who were moving into the house. They were a Vietnamese family and were supposedly friends of Mom's. So I called them and talked to the husband, explaining my situation and asking if I could stay at the house for another month. He told me that I couldn't because they needed to move in. Then I asked if I could live with them for a month until I could find another place to live. Even though the thought of living with them would have been uncomfortable for me since I really didn't know them, I was desperate. However, the answer again was "no". I couldn't believe it. How could people just be that cold and basically kick someone out in the street? However, I kept praying and searching and finally, I learned that the ministers in the congregation had gotten together and found a place for me to live. It was with a divorced single lady named Maria whom I had seen and met at church before, and who had a one bedroom apartment. They had asked her if she could take me in for a few months until I found my own place and I would help with some of the rent. She didn't have much but at least it was a roof over my head.

So I moved in with Maria who lived not too far from my new job at the Stationary store. Her apartment was in a small complex and was on the second level. I didn't have much to move fortunately and some of the friends from church helped me. I did bring the small orange cushioned sofa, since Maria didn't have a couch, and slept on it in the living room because she only had one bedroom. It was now summer and the temperature was getting over 110 degrees outside and being on the second story of a building made it extremely hot inside the apartment. Yet, Maria would not turn on the air conditioning because she wanted to save on her electric bill.

One Saturday afternoon, I was taking a nap on the small orange sofa that was positioned right underneath the living room window. Maria was sleeping in her bedroom with a fan on. Something made me wake up and when I got up, I felt really sick and nauseous. I also felt really hot, disoriented and dizzy. I began to slowly walk to Maria's room and knocked on her door. There was no response so I knocked a little louder. Finally, she told me to come in. When I opened up her door, I began to tell her how sick I was feeling and before I could finish what I was saying, I fainted and dropped to the floor. Maria jumped out of bed and helped me sit up and asked if I was okay. I told her that I felt really hot and sick so she got some water and gave it to me to drink. After that, Maria began to use the air conditioner.

After living with Maria for about three months, I moved in with another family who had two older adult daughters who came back home to live with them. Their daughters had lived in the Bay Area but missed their parents, so they wanted to move back home with them. Victor and Adriana had a three bedroom home where each of the girls had their own rooms; however, they converted their living room into a huge bedroom where their oldest daughter Loretta and I slept. Loretta slept on the twin bed that doubled as a couch during the day and I slept on the trundle bed that was tucked away every morning under Loretta's bed. So I would pay Victor and Adriana rent each month for living in their home. I lived with the Flores family for approximately two years before moving into an apartment with another roommate. From that point on, I was able to maintain a roof over my head and things just kept falling into place for me. It hadn't occurred to me until many years later that I could have been homeless, but I was thankful that through the church, someone was looking after me.

# 18 Drifting Without a Dream or Purpose

Dad was out in the garage with the hood of the car up. He was working on the engine as he normally would when he wanted to get out of the house after an argument with Mom. Sometimes, he would show James things about the engine. This time, James wasn't around so I decided to watch what Dad was doing. As I quietly leaned over the side of the car, staring down at the different parts of the engine, I began asking Dad some questions. After just a few minutes, he said, "You don't need to know any of this stuff. You just need to learn how to help Mom cook and clean and then find some man to marry so he can take care of you." Well that shut me up really quick. I looked at Dad without knowing what to say. However, I did wonder what he meant by "help" Mom. Why, I was doing everything! I thought that if he was trying to teach me a lesson on being a submissive wife, it was ironic that his own wife wasn't being submissive to him. According to Catholicism, the wife is supposed to be submissive to the husband but it was very apparent that Mom ruled the roost in the house.

Even though Mom and I never talked about me getting married, I felt that I was already groomed to be a slave if I were to get married. I had wondered why she never talked to me about it because she had gotten married at a very young age. Then I would see many youths in my church get married young also. However, I knew that I was not anywhere near ready for marriage. Why should I go from being a slave to my family to being a slave to a man? That was what I thought marriage would have been like for me since that was all my parents ever aspired for me.

Instead, I wanted to prove to myself that I could support myself without help from my parents, a man, or anyone else. Even though I didn't really know how I was going to do that. As I watched my parents ask my brothers what they wanted to be, it made me feel sad that they never asked me what I wanted to become when I got older. James always said he wanted to be a pilot. I've forgotten what my two other brothers said they wanted to be but they were big and lofty things. It never occurred to me that because my parents never asked me what I wanted to do or become, I didn't know how to believe in myself, I didn't know how to dream and I didn't know what my purpose in life was. I didn't realize how important that was until many years later.

All I knew was that I couldn't wait to grow up and get a job so I could move away from my family. In high school, most of the classes I took were geared toward office jobs or accounting so I thought that was the direction I would go. Although the school counselors encouraged me to go to college, I didn't think I could go because Dad had told me that he wasn't going to pay for it and I never thought I could qualify for any scholarships or grants. Then in church, nobody ever encouraged me to go to college either. Instead, I just heard lessons about being a spiritual person, how to live a life that was pleasing to God, and telling others about your faith. Even though going to church taught me a lot of great values on how to be a good person, how to treat other people, and how to live my life with a clean conscience, I never truly knew what I wanted to be or do.

My parents' neglect of not recognizing or nurturing the potential I had in any area, whether it be music, art, academics or any other field, and also the lack of guidance from church, made me realize that I hadn't really learned how to think for myself. I never thought about what *I* really wanted and I didn't know how to dream. I thought my purpose was to share my faith with other people to make this world a better place. It was just a matter of surviving and paying the bills and not a matter of whether I was happy at the job. I just didn't know any better.

I also came to realize that I went from having a very rigid and strict upbringing at home to finding and attracting a faith that in many ways was restrictive as well. There were so many things that were prohibited, or perhaps that was what I had the tendency to hear and focus on since that was the programming that I came with. While I thought I was applying the things I learned, I saw others in the church behaving and conducting themselves in ways that were not approved of, according to what I had been taught. I realized that some of the kids that grew up with the training and teachings of the church were the worst ones. The saying, "The Preachers' daughters are always the worst" and the term "hypocritical" certainly seemed to apply to them.

Nevertheless, I will always be grateful for the things I learned in church, like what love really feels like, the importance of being honest in everything that you do, and to treat others the way you would want to be treated. The values that I learned in church also helped me to be able to get along with everyone around me and prevented me from going down a destructive path, which I easily could have done. But that was not to be my fate.

One day, when I was working at the stationary store, a lady who was a social worker came in. I didn't remember her but somehow she remembered me and my previous case. As I was ringing her up at the cash register, she asked me how I was doing. She said to me as if she was impressed, "Wow, I didn't expect you to do so well. Most foster kids don't do very well after they leave the system."

I looked at her without knowing what to say. What do you mean foster kids don't do that well? After she left, I thought about it more but because I was not in contact with any of the other kids from the Grays or the receiving home, I had no idea where those kids were or what they were doing these days. I guess I was fortunate but I didn't feel I had a choice. It was a matter of survival for me. I *had* to get a job since there was nobody around to bail me out. What else was I supposed to do?

Now that I was living on my own, in that I was no longer living with my family, I was enjoying the freedom of doing pretty much whatever I wanted. I had a big network of friends through church and we would do a lot of fun things together like hiking, camping, traveling, sight-seeing and touring big cities like San Francisco, San Diego, and New York. I was finally able to discover who I was and what I liked to do instead of having to take care of someone else. I never thought that I would like to do something like hiking. Because I wanted to do more things and eventually have my own place instead of relying on a roommate, I began to look for jobs that paid more. I got bored easily and was always seeking the next challenge, which included a little better pay.

Finally, I realized that if I wanted to get a job that paid more, I would need a college degree. So I decided to take evening classes, which required a lot of energy. At times, when I took two classes at a time, worked full-time, and went to service meetings through church three times a week, I became so exhausted that I thought I would drop dead. I didn't have the energy that most people had. I admired those people who could work full-time and go to school full-time or those single mothers who worked, went to school and also took care of their children.

Mary Jane and Robert saw how I was struggling to go to school and work full-time so they told me that I should go work for the prison system. They told me that the California Department of Corrections (CDC) was the fastest growing state department and that because I was smart and had good work ethics, I would be able to progress up the ladder within the CDC and not have to have a degree. This was because of the Three Strikes You're Out law that put anyone away for life after three felonies. They also told me about the great benefits from working for a state department. He also mentioned the ability to transfer all over the state, since there were several prisons throughout California.

"Once you get into the system, you'll be able to transfer all over the state," he said as a matter of fact.

I looked up at Robert and said, "Well, that's easy for you to say. You have a wife that will move with you. It's easy when you have a family to move around like that but when it's just you, it's a lot harder."

Robert had no idea what I was talking about. He was a guy and I learned that men are just more logical. He didn't understand how hard it was for me emotionally to move from place to place by myself. After my family moved away, I had moved five times between renting a room and having roommates. Then, when I moved to Fresno for a job, I moved five times during the five and a half years I lived there. It was no roommate, roommate, no roommate, roommate. Needless to say, when I finally moved to the Central Coast, to work for a maximum security, Level IV State Prison, I had had it. If anyone mentioned the word "move", I thought I would have a nervous breakdown.

One of the biggest reasons why I moved around so much was for employment. I hadn't realized that I was doing exactly what my father had done, which was to move to where the employment was. The location didn't matter and it wasn't a question of whether you would be happy there or not. It was where the money was. Dad would often tell me, "Well, you got a go where the job is." Sadly, I don't think Dad really knew what happiness is. To him, job security and a monthly paycheck equaled happiness.

So I took Robert and Mary Jane's advice and left my job in administration for an entry-level position at the women's prison, located about 30 minutes out of town. Even though I had to take a slight cut in pay, Robert and Mary Jane told me it would be worth it in the long run. I worked at the women's prison for two and a half years before transferring to the men's prison due to a job promotion. Although I wasn't crazy about living in the farming community where the prison was located and had given up on my dream of living in San Diego, my fear of an emotional meltdown of making another major move to an area where I didn't know anyone was too great. Therefore, I stayed working at the men's prison and living in the agricultural town for far too long.

When I first got the assignment and promotion of being a Vocational Instructor at the Level IV, Maximum Security Prison, I was scared to death. I wanted the position since it would be better pay and certainly be more challenging than working in an office as an Office Technician. Yet, despite my fears, I took on the challenge. I had learned from Mom how to hide my true feelings and act as if nothing bothered me. Nevertheless, the first year of that assignment was extremely challenging and difficult. It made me wonder if I had made the right decision. I heard when I first worked at the women's prison, that women inmates were worse than the male inmates because they were much more manipulative. However, I soon found that the men were just as manipulative and conning. Especially when they knew you were a new employee. Somehow, they had a way of knowing. They had plenty of time on their hands to watch and study correctional officers and other staff. Also, since I was one of the youngest and one of the few female instructors in the prison, they put me through so much "hell" by testing me and pushing my buttons. In addition, most of these men had little respect for authority, let alone a woman in authority. Since many of them probably were abusive towards their girlfriends or wives on the outside, many of them had a difficult time following my directions. But, I held my ground and the results were phenomenal.

Certainly, there was great satisfaction in seeing the changes in the inmate students I had taught. Somehow, I had taken an unruly, loud, and chaotic classroom full of disrespectful, unfocused students and turned them into the quietest and most diligent learners. It took over a year to do that but one day, when I was sitting in my office and looking out my office window into the classroom, I noticed that every student's head was faced down as they were reading and studying their school work. It was so quiet, you could hear a pin drop. I sat there and thought, *Wow! I did this*! I had no idea I could do this or have this type of effect on them. It was an amazing transformation in attitude and behavior.

Even though I had formed a reputation out in the "Yard" that I was a "bitch", I knew that I had really earned the respect of my students. One student told me that when he would hear other inmates (inmates who weren't programming, meaning they didn't have a job assignment or they weren't enrolled in school) out in the yard talk about me, he would simply tell them, "All you have to do is do what she says and you'll be fine. She's really not that bad." I realized though that the reason I was so effective was because I really cared about these students and they knew it. I wasn't there just to collect a paycheck and I treated them with respect. I treated them as if they were a human being, regardless of their past or the reason why they ended up in prison. I didn't know what they were in for and I didn't want to know. Sometimes I would hear them talk to each other about their stories of how they came to prison but usually, I would just tune them out. It was better that I didn't know.

So as it turned out, Robert and Mary Jane were right. I continued to advance and get raises while working at the prison and despite having done well financially in investing in the real estate market, I was miserable. I learned that money alone cannot make you happy. What's truly important are the people in your life, for without healthy, meaningful, and supportive relationships, the nice home and the nice car are meaningless and empty in and of themselves.

# 19 A "Happy" Family Reunion

My brother James, his girlfriend Kelly, and I arrived on May 20th to Washington to visit Mom, Dad, and Dennis. James and Kelly came from Alaska and I came up from California. It was almost like a family reunion except Luc wasn't there. He had been on his own ever since he joined the Air Force and rarely kept in touch with the family. Even though I felt my parents were hardest on me and that I was the black sheep of the family, it seemed that Luc was really the black sheep of the family since he didn't get along with any of us siblings.

Things started out fine and it was nice to see Dennis. He had grown up a lot in the last six years. He was ten when they moved away and now he was sixteen. After James left to go to college on the main land of Alaska, Dennis was the only child left at home so he got to do and have a lot of things that Luc, James, and I couldn't do. He was able to play a musical instrument and received more "toys". You would think that I would have gotten jealous of him for getting all these material things but I wasn't. I was glad that my parents eased up on Dennis and were able to give him more, at least materially. However, I learned from Dennis that Mom was really hard on him. He shared how Mom would get on him about things or try to restrict him from doing certain things and how angry he would get at Mom. I wasn't surprised. With the other kids gone, there was no one left to target, except for Dennis.

When we first got there, my brothers and I talked about what we wanted to do. Touring Seattle was at the top of our list, along with going up to British Columbia. However, Mom had her own plans for us. Even though James and I had been on our own for a while, Mom wanted to still control us. So we acquiesced and went along with her idea of going up to Vancouver to visit one of her friends. At first, we thought that it would be fun to tour Vancouver. However, when we got there, we went straight to her friend's apartment where Mom, her friend, her friend's wife, and Dad sat all afternoon talking. It was mostly Mom, her friend, and her friend's wife that were talking because they were speaking in Vietnamese. Although her friend could speak some English so he was able to talk to Dad as well.

Her friend and his wife didn't have very many furnishings, so my brothers, Kelly, and I would stand around in the apartment and looked down into the city from the window. We shared how we were disappointed with the trip since it was obvious that Mom wanted to show us off to her friend. Mom had met him when we were living in the Philippines and since James and I were so young, we didn't remember who he was. As they sat and talked, Mom's friend kept bringing beer after beer out for him and Dad to drink. After a while, there were well over a dozen bottles of beer that were drunk by him and Dad. That was the first time I had really seen what James had told me before about Dad, how he was an alcoholic. I became concerned that Dad wouldn't be able to drive.

As they continued talking, James and I discussed how we would confront Mom. We wanted her to know that we didn't want or need to be controlled by her anymore. We were adults now and had been on our own so we were capable of making our own decisions and should be able to do what we want. We were also going to tell her how we were neglected by her growing up, how she and Dad didn't raise us, the maids did. Then after the maids, we raised ourselves because she and Dad were rarely ever home.

So the next day, when James and I discussed with Dennis what we wanted to do while we were up in Washington, we asked our parents if we could borrow the car to go sightseeing. Amazingly, Mom wouldn't allow us to borrow one of the cars for us to go into Seattle. She made such a big deal about her wanting us to do what she wanted, even though she didn't say what they were, that it was frustrating beyond belief. While Dad and Dennis went to the store, James and I decided to confront Mom and told her all the things that had been on our minds. Mom of course became angry and upset and began to wail, saying that we didn't love her. She was obviously blowing things out of proportion. It made me feel sick to my stomach. Then, on top of that, she attempted to inflict a guilt trip on us. But I wouldn't have it because I knew she was being manipulative. And I just didn't have the desire or loving feeling to comfort her. However, James walked over to Mom and put his hand on her back and told her, "Of course we love you. It's just that we're adults now and we don't need to be told what to do anymore." Of course Mom didn't get it. How could she? She was so unreasonable in her obsession to control that there was no way anyone could reason with her.

When Dad and Dennis got back home, we explained to him what happened. Dad became upset of course and tried to talk to Mom into letting us borrow the car. Mom still wouldn't have it but in the end, Dad told us we could. So the rest of the week, James, Kelly, Dennis, and I explored Seattle, visiting the aquarium and Space Needle. We also went back up to British Columbia and visited the zoo and other attractions. It felt good to reconnect with my two younger brothers. Mom and Dad decided to just stay back since there wasn't enough room to fit all of us in the car. Besides, Mom was too upset to do anything with us. So once again, instead of being able to move forward, let go, and grow, she wanted to hang on to her old ways of wanting to control us. Fortunately, Dad was reasonable enough to let us take the car so we could have some semblance of a happy family reunion and vacation.

When I got back home to California, I was fortunately able to resume my life with the friends from church. I was glad to be back around more loving people and away from the dysfunction of Mom. Then sadly, on June 20$^{th}$, exactly one month later from the day James and I arrived in Washington to visit the family, I received the call that nobody is ever prepared for. Even though the relationship between me and Mom was very challenging and extremely toxic, it was still a devastating call. When the phone rang, my roommate picked up and handed me the phone and told me, "It's your dad."

"Hello?" I answered.

"Eden, your mother passed," the voice on the other side said calmly.

"What?!" I asked shocked. Instantly, tears ran down my face. I felt warm and weak in the knees. I couldn't believe it.

"What do you mean she passed? How?" I asked incredulously and with my voice shaking.

"Well, she had another heart attack and this time, she didn't make it," Dad said in a low tone.

He explained further that when she had her first heart attack when I was 11 and had to be hospitalized, the doctor had diagnosed her with a rare heart disease called Takayasu Disease, which is the chronic inflammation of the large blood vessels. This restricts the blood flow to the body, which eventually leads to heart failure. Fortunately, it wasn't hereditary. At the time, the doctor's prognosis was that she would only live another five years. I never knew. It was something my parents never told my brothers or me. They kept so much from us. I became upset. How could they keep this from us? On the one hand, I had to grow up very fast because I was given so many adult responsibilities but on the other hand, I was treated as if I was too young to understand adult experiences and was sheltered from many things. It was so confusing.

I always had in the back of my mind that Mom could die in a few years. I would see the large bruise-like discoloration marks on her legs and her pale and pasty looking skin. But it was always in a couple years. Well, those couple of years finally came. Even so, it was still a shock and a devastating blow. She was only 41. I cried for several days. Losing Mom was one of the hardest things I had ever gone through. It gave me the ability to truly empathize with other people who have lost loved ones. Some friends would say, "Well, it's not like you were really that close to her," as if that was going to console me. I would look at them in disbelief and reply, "Still, she was my mother and it's still hurts." It took me about two years to fully recover from her loss.

When I went back up to Washington to attend Mom's funeral, Luc was there as well. It was awkward to see him but I did my best to show him kindness and love. We hadn't talked since the last time he verbally attacked me, claiming I wanted to live in a utopia, because I wanted to put our past behind us and move forward in a more loving and kind way. Since my brothers and I stayed at Dad's place, I quickly fell back into the motherly role again of cooking for the family. One day, Dad said to me with a hurt look on his face, "I wish you could move up here." I couldn't believe he had said that. I knew it was hard on him, but it was hard on *all* of us and for him to lean on me for emotional support was just too much. He wasn't there for me and now he wants me to be there for him? It felt weird and strange. There was no way I was going to move to Washington.

I immediately thought, *Why, so I could cook and clean for you?* but remained silent.

Dad rarely talked about Mom when she was alive. The few times I tried to tell him how she was treating me, he would just brush off my fears and concerns, which made me realize that I couldn't go to him for support. He seemed to be in denial. I wondered how he could not see what was going on. But he did see and he did know. He just didn't want to talk about it. One evening, while I was making dinner for the family, Dad came into the kitchen. "You know, I hate to say this but it's kind of a relief," he said calmly about Mom's passing.

I looked at him in without saying a word. I knew exactly what he meant. How sad to think that Mom's human existence was mainly filled with the intention to make others miserable, especially her own family, the people she should have loved and protected the most, because she didn't know how to love herself. And while most people in that situation would have felt guilty and blame themselves for possibly causing Mom's death by confronting her and getting her so upset that it resulted in a fatal heart attack, I didn't. I refused to blame myself. I had felt and received enough blame and shame in my life up to that point that I couldn't take on any more guilt, nor could I take the responsibility of being the cause of her death. I had heard somewhere along the way that our emotions can cause illnesses in the body and somehow knew that Mom had caused her own death.

# 20 From Dreams of Abandonment to Dreams of Love

I was in a dark place. I don't know where I was but someone was slowly walking towards me. As I stood still, I saw that it was a woman dressed in a gown. Her eyes were bright green and glowing. That was the only color I could see in that dark place. Everything else was shades of black and gray. I was frightened and tried to move but I couldn't. Then I woke up with my heart racing and my breath, hard and shallow. I was about seven when I had that dream about Mom. It was very frightening and yet when I awoke from it, I knew right away why I'd had it. Really, it wasn't that difficult to figure out. It seemed that Mom was always looking down at me with disdain, resentment, and anger. There was nothing I could ever do to please her. And this resentment and anger from her translated into her being a monster in my dreams. I had other dreams about Mom in my childhood. Mostly they were about her leaving me, like the one I mentioned in an earlier chapter where I would be on my knees crying and begging her not to leave me. Those dreams weren't too hard to interpret either. There was no bond or love between us. Mom had abandoned me emotionally before I was even born. I was an unwanted child.

As a teenager and into my adult years, I would continue to dream about Mom. Even after her death I continued to have dreams about her. Usually there would be a struggle between us and sometimes we would be involved in a physical altercation. I would wake up feeling tense and frustrated. Over time however, the frequency of my dreams about her slowly diminished and when I did dream about her, they were very peaceful. We would be walking side by side and actually just be talking like a normal mother and daughter would. How strange I felt after awakening from those types of dreams of Mom. I would say, "Of course that could only happen in my dreams. If she were alive, we could never have this type of conversation or be able to get along this way." But those types of dreams continued and I began to realize that I had finally let go. I had finally forgiven her and no longer harbored any resentment. I knew that I had to do it for my own sake. I couldn't continue hurting myself and carrying the burden of anger.

After a while, I began to accept and appreciate those types of dreams about Mom. The few people I shared those dreams with, the ones that knew of our previous relationship told me that Mom was trying to reconcile things with me. While I don't know if that is what actually occurred, I do know that a huge weight was lifted when I was finally able to forgive her.

I recall the day when this occurred. I was living in Fresno and I was at home in my apartment. I got to thinking about Mom and through the anger that I felt for how she mistreated me growing up, it suddenly occurred to me that Mom must've been through so much pain herself. I had learned from Dad that my grandmother, was especially hard on Mom for some reason. She was the younger of the two girls in her family and had lost two of her three brothers in the war. Then she lost her father at a young age also. Perhaps that is why she married so young to look for a man to take care of her. Knowing that, I was able to really dig deep and placed myself in her shoes and in her embodiment. There is where I was able to see it from her perspective. There was so much pain and grief. Pain for all the losses and pain for not feeling loved. This didn't justify her actions and that wasn't what I was looking for. I wasn't looking for justification. I was looking for understanding and to be able to see things from her perspective. The pain and anger was so great yet I allowed myself to feel it. As I sat on my sofa, I cried and cried and cried. I don't know how long I sat there crying but at some point, I finally let go.

After that, I began to have dreams of Mom being supportive of me. In one dream, she invited me to go have dinner with her but I was too busy working. I told her that I couldn't go so she came back and brought dinner for me. In my dream, her bringing me dinner was nothing unusual, although I was very appreciative of what she did. Also in that dream, it felt as if we had always had that type of relationship. When I awoke, I felt awestruck and at the same time liberated. I realized that I had finally crossed that bridge to healing myself. Then one day, I dreamt that she had put her arms around me as we were slowly walking side by side and talking, then she turned to me and said, "I love you." She was offering me support through whatever I was going through. In turn, I said to her, "I love you too Mom."

# AFTERWORD

Many years have gone by since my mother's passing. About a year after her death, my father remarried. My stepmother, who was one of my mother's friends, is one of the kindest, warmest, and loving people I know. Anne is nearly the opposite of my mother when she was alive and I had wondered how they could have been friends. As I have gotten to know Anne, she explained that she and my mother were friends through church and that they really didn't do a lot together. Anne truly displays and shows unconditional love in her dealings with everyone around her. Hence, my father and the rest of the family are blessed to have her in our lives.

When I was nearing the completion of this writing, I had a conversation with my father about my mother to get more information for this memoir. We haven't always been able to talk in the manner that we do today. One reason is that I no longer wanted to talk about the past since I didn't feel it would serve me. I preferred to keep my mind focused on the present and on my future. I had also assumed that my father didn't want to talk about the past either. Surprisingly, my father began to open up about his experiences with my mother. One thing that I never knew was that my mother was actually 15 when she had my older brother and 17 when she had me. All my life, I had thought she was 17 and 19 because that was the story I was told by my childhood friend. Because that was the story my mother told *her* friends. Learning that she had her birth certificate changed so she could be older put things in an entirely different perspective for me. As if 17 wasn't young enough, being only 15 is nearly tragic, in my opinion. While it was common for Vietnamese women to marry and have babies at a young age, I don't believe starting at 15 was the norm.

My dad also revealed to me that he almost left my mother in Vietnam where they met, even though they already had a child together, my younger brother James. He didn't go into specifics of her behavior but evidently, she was already showing signs of dysfunction. He also said, "She never should've had kids." This was in reference to her being extremely young when she became a mother and also because she had no concept of what being a mother entailed. I heard from both my father and stepmother Anne that my mother would say, "Friend number one. Family number two," meaning that her friends came before her family. Her behavior certainly demonstrated that value. However, hearing my father make that statement was startling. To think that if she never had any children, then I wouldn't be here! I wouldn't be having the joyful, meaningful, and even blissful life that I do now. Even though earlier in my journey, I felt that I didn't ask to be here. However, I now realize that I am here for a reason and a purpose, just as you are here for a reason and a purpose.

**The Inner Hero**

I have come to learn that the inner hero is the light inside each and every one of us. It's the force, energy, and spirit that wants us to not only survive but thrive. It's the part of us that wants only the best for us so we can live a life of happiness, bliss, euphoria, peace, love, and truth. No matter who you are, I am certain you have overcome obstacles and adversities in your journey and past. Can you think of those times and moments? Just as I have, you've had to tap into that part of you to get you through those critical and difficult times. Certainly, having the encouragement and support of family and friends is helpful to get us through those challenging times. Perhaps your faith has helped you as well. However, during those times when you felt there was nobody there for you, who was there to help you? It was your inner hero, the one that will always be there to rescue and save you, and guide you through that dark tunnel.

In the Foreword, my dear friend and mentor Earlene Vining mentioned that I exhibited a confidence that made me stand out in the class. That made me realize that throughout my life, I exhibited, at times, a confidence that I never knew I had. I would marvel and wonder where this confidence came from despite my low self-esteem and self-image during those times. In the *Law of Success*, original 1925 edition, Napoleon Hill mentioned that after you reach a certain "point in the process of your evolution, you will have sufficient knowledge of the real source from which you are drawing your power to give full credit to *Infinite Intelligence* for all that you previously credited to your Self-Confidence." When I read that sentence, I came to realize that my self-confidence was that Infinite Intelligence or inner hero that I had tapped into. Whatever name you choose to use, it is certainly a power that we all have.

On the other hand, there is another power or invisible force that is designed to keep you numb, detached, in the dark, and to keep you from discovering your true potential. It is pervasive, insidious, and permeates all areas of our lives, and can be disguised as so called friends, family members, churches, coworkers, schools, the media, certain authority figures, and even ourselves, our egos. While these people and entities may not be aware or conscious that they are preventing us from our true identity, gifts, and powers, nevertheless they play an active role in keeping us from recognizing and being aware of who we really are.

Over the years, when I thought about writing my biography, I heard many people say that writing one's biography would be cathartic, therapeutic, and healing. However, when I embarked on this journey to write this memoir, I didn't think I needed to write for my own healing. I had already forgiven those that needed it, including myself. My initial purpose in writing was to help others heal. Yet something happened as I began to put pen to paper. A shift took place. A weight had lifted and I began to feel lighter. Evidently, healing never stops.

I have also come to understand that no matter how positive you may want to be and no matter how hard you work at thinking positive, in order to create a more fulfilling life, positive thinking is not enough. While it's an excellent start and a necessity, you must also clear out the negative charges and memories that are stored in your body and in your mind. Until you are clear from these negative thoughts and memories, it will be difficult, if not impossible, to truly create the kind of life you desire and deserve. This doesn't mean that you've forgotten your past, but that these memories no longer have power over you. As you can see, I still remember much of my past and many memories came to me for the sole purpose of writing this book. But I am no longer affected and controlled by them.

So I share this story with you to show you that no matter what you've gone through, you have the ability to clear these negative memories and charges out of your mind and body to create new neural pathways that will create new positive experiences that you desire. You also have the ability to now look back on your own story and see where you have been your own hero.

In recent years I have discovered a few things that have helped me clear away these negative charges and also helped me reach a level of optimum health and healing. While there is still room to grow and heal, I have found that these have worked better and faster than anything else I have tried. I have listed them in the back of the book for your reference.

## Where I am today

If it were not for the CD series called "Your Wish Is Your Command", I would not be where I am today and the person I am today. I would not have met the extraordinary people who have come into my life and I would not have been able to achieve this dream of writing my memoir. Because of the message and information I learned from the CDs, I began to learn how to think for myself and believe that I could be, do, and have anything and everything I want in my life. Learning, then believing that I can achieve my dreams is what I have come to realize is the truth. I have also come to realize that the negative and limiting messages that came from my mother and others, including myself, were a lie. If you find yourself surrounded by those who give you those negative messages and who don't support your dreams, you may want to reconsider associating with them.

Because I am a very different person than I was four years ago, my relationship with my father has improved dramatically. While I had long just accepted him for who he is and how he is, I never thought that by *me* changing, it would change my relationship with him for the better. Also, now I am saying "yes" to myself instead of "no" when it comes to learning or creating something new. Today, I have the support of thousands of friends from all over the world who tell me I *can* reach for the stars and achieve all my dreams. I am diving into new territories of creating art, music, learning a new language, and traveling to places I've never been to before. And this is only the beginning. While this may be the end of this writing and where this part of the story ends, it is not the end of my journey and work. There is still more to come and I hope you'll join me in the adventures ahead.

# REFERENCES

1.  For mental and emotional balancing instruments go to:

    www.ichingsystemsmembers.com

2.  To clear negative emotional charges in your body, I recommend getting Bio-Energetic Synchronization Treatments (B.E.S.T.) on a regular basis. To learn more about B.E.S.T. and to find a practitioner near you, go to:

    www.morter.com

    Or you can call Morter Health Systems at (800) 874-1478.

3.  To learn more about how you can Be, Do, and Have more in your life through the Law of Attraction and beyond, go to:

    http://edenrein.myginclub.com/

4.  To help you learn more about who you really are and how you can love yourself more through meditation and yoga, I highly recommend learning from world renowned Master Yoga Teacher (the Teacher of the Teachers) Aadil Palkhivala and his highly intuitive meditation teacher and wife, Savitri, at the Alive and Shine Center in Bellevue, Washington, U.S. Please go to:

    www.aliveandshinecenter.com

5.  For simply the best whole food supplements and herbal formulas to fill in your nutritional deficiencies, go to:

    www.edenrein.com/healthyliving

For more information or if you have any questions, please contact the author at www.edenrein.com.

10653229R00153

Made in the USA
San Bernardino, CA
22 April 2014